# Comparative Securities Law

Providing a clear introduction to securities laws and how they are applied in different countries, this book compares the enaction and enforcement of securities laws in Kuwait, the UK and the USA.

It explores the philosophy behind securities laws and methods of application in Kuwait, the US and UK to consider the benefits and the risks associated with trading in securities. Using case studies from each jurisdiction, the book takes a comparative approach to examining the different laws that have been enacted with a view to addressing problems that have developed on stock exchanges and in corporate governance. It details the different regulatory authorities in the different countries and the rules and laws that are used to ensure that markets continue to trade and that investors are protected, highlighting the differences in common law, civil law and Middle Eastern law approaches to securities and the bearing of these in the modern securities trade.

Contributing to the general discipline of securities law and providing valuable insights into Middle Eastern law, the US and UK, this book will be of interest to students of international law, scholars, policy makers and government officials.

**Abdullah Alshebli** is Assistant Professor of Law in Kuwait.

T0347948

# Comparative Securities Law

Perspectives from Kuwait,
the UK and US

**Abdullah Alshebli**

LONDON AND NEW YORK

First published 2022
by Routledge
4 Park Square, Milton Park, Abingdon, Oxon OX14 4RN

and by Routledge
605 Third Avenue, New York, NY 10158

*Routledge is an imprint of the Taylor & Francis Group, an informa business*

© 2022 Abdullah Alshebli

*British Library Cataloguing-in-Publication Data*
A catalogue record for this book is available from the British Library

*Library of Congress Cataloging-in-Publication Data*
A catalog record has been requested for this book

ISBN: 978-1-032-29503-9 (hbk)
ISBN: 978-1-032-29505-3 (pbk)
ISBN: 978-1-003-30187-5 (ebk)

DOI: 10.4324/9781003301875

Typeset in Times New Roman
by Deanta Global Publishing Services, Chennai, India

# Contents

# Introduction

Securities law is the study of all laws and regulations related to the issuing of and dealing in securities. Whilst the topic of securities law is regulated differently from country to country, it typically falls under the heading of financial or commercial law.

This book aims to give a basic, simple, and clear understanding of the different types of securities in Kuwait, the United Kingdom (UK), and the United States (US). It considers the topic of securities laws as enacted in these countries and the methods used to enforce them. Where possible, examples of situations where the laws were applied are discussed and explained in a way that the first-time reader can comprehend the complexities of the subject. Issues relating to corporate governance and the proper conduct of boards of directors, investors, and securities traders are also considered.

Furthermore, a basic comparison of the different legal systems and laws in the countries of Kuwait, the UK, and the US are set out in the book. This explanation highlights the difference between the common law, civil law, and Middle Eastern law approaches to securities. This has a bearing on the promulgation and enforcement of laws that are needed in the modern securities trade.

The main objective of the book is to discuss the philosophy behind securities laws and methods of application in Kuwait, the UK, and the US. It considers the benefits of trading in securities and the risks associated therewith. Specific reference is made to the different kinds of laws that have been enacted with a view to addressing problems that have developed on stock exchanges and in corporate governance. Furthermore, the book details the different regulatory authorities in these countries and the rules and laws that are used to ensure that markets continue to trade and that investors are protected.

DOI: 10.4324/9781003301875-1

This book has been prepared as a guide to students, scholars, policymakers, government officials, and law enforcement personnel. It sets out what securities laws are and how they are applied in the Kuwait legal system. It is hoped that it will motivate the reader to further study the subject of securities laws.

# 1 What Are Securities?

This chapter gives a clear and simple definition of what securities are, which provides the foundation of the book. The purpose of securities, the benefits of trading in securities, and the risks associated with securities are set out in detail. In the second part of the chapter, different types of securities are discussed and examples of each are provided.

## 1.1 What Are Securities?

To understand the subject of securities law one needs to appreciate what is meant by the term securities. 'Securities' is a broad term that refers to any form of ownership or beneficial interest in a business entity. A security is a tradeable financial asset that can further be categorised into debt securities (e.g., banknotes, bonds, and debentures) and equity securities (e.g., common stocks).

Securities law relates to the group of laws that seeks to regulate the sale or transfer of these securities or business interests. Typically, securities are investments traded on a stock market. They can include such items as:

- *Bonds*: a creditor relationship with a government body or a firm (bonds, *sukuk*,[1] and debt securities).[2]

---

1 An alternative financial investment to bonds are *sukuk* instruments, which perform an equivalent function to bonds and loans used in the Western financial system, but use Sharia-compliant financial instruments. They are structured to pay a return linked to the assets that the bond has funded, so that they are not paid in a conventional sense. They are a form of asset-based and profit-sharing instrument. Iain G MacNeil, *An Introduction to the Law on Financial Investment* (2nd edn, Hart Publishing Ltd 2012) 146.
2 Debt securities are proof of a monetary debt which must be repaid according to certain terms that define the interest rate and maturity/renewal data. <www.imf.org/external/np/sta/wgsd/pdf/051309.pdf>.

DOI: 10.4324/9781003301875-2

- *Equities*: an ownership position in a publicly traded company's shares.[3]
- *Derivatives*: rights to ownership as represented by an option.[4]

Each of these categories can furthermore consist of different types as will be discussed in the following.[5]

Securities in the US are defined by the Securities Act of 1933. Section 2 (a)(1) of this Act defines securities as follows:

> (1) The term 'security' means any note, stock, treasury stock, security future, security-based swap, bond, debenture, evidence of indebtedness, certificate of interest or participation in any profit-sharing agreement, collateral-trust certificate, pre-organisation certificate or subscription, transferable share, investment contract, voting-trust certificate, certificate of deposit for a security, fractional undivided interest in oil, gas, or other mineral rights, any put, call, straddle, option, or privilege on any security, certificate of deposit, or group or index of securities (including any interest therein or based on the value thereof), or any put, call, straddle, option, or privilege entered into on a national securities exchange relating to foreign currency, or, in general, any interest or instrument commonly known as a 'security', or any certificate of interest or participation in, temporary or interim certificate for, receipt for, guarantee of, or warrant or right to subscribe to or purchase, any of the foregoing.

From the above definition, it is clear that the term 'security' includes several different items and has a fairly wide application. However, it should be noted that in general, the term applies to stocks and bonds as traded on the stock exchange.

---

3 Three rights are given to an investor who buys shares. The first is the right to vote. The second is the right to take delivery of a corporation's residual cash flows. The third is the right, after all claimants have been paid, to the residual assets in liquidation. Stephen J Choi and A C Pritchard, *Securities Regulation: The Essentials* (Aspen Publishers 2008) 10.

4 The purchaser has an option rather than an obligation to buy or sell, so the consumer buys the option against a sum of money. The premium paid is the highest loss that the purchaser of an option can suffer. MacNeil (n 1) 154.

5 Each of the securities has advantages and disadvantages. For example, one of the advantages of issuing shares is that the issuing companies do not have to repay the borrowers' money except in the event of liquidation.

### 1.1.1 *Purpose of Securities*

Securities allow an entity issuing them (known as the issuer) to attract people or institutions willing to invest money (known as the investor). By issuing securities, the entity can raise capital or gain investment in a specific project. For investors, buying and later selling securities allows them to increase the value of the money invested, or to earn dividends paid out over time.

The most well-known type of securities is publicly traded shares. The terms 'stocks', 'shares',[6] and 'equities' are synonyms for each other and are terms used to describe units of ownership in a company. The owner (known as a shareholder) has a right to a part of the company's earnings if a dividend payment is made, as well as voting rights.

### 1.1.2 *Benefits of Securities*

The main aim of investors is to increase the value of their money. By investing in debt securities, such as bonds or by buying shares or equity, investors can grow the value of their investments. In most cases, investors aim to improve their financial position through capital gain (growth),[7] or income (interest payments of dividends),[8] whilst retaining the ability to convert their investments to cash quickly (in the case of shares).[9,10]

Owners of ordinary shares share in the profits of the company (dividends), vote in company decision-making, and have the right to attend an

---

6 There are different types or categories of shares, such as ordinary shares and preference shares. These can be further categorised into deferred ordinary shares, non-voting ordinary shares, redeemable shares, preference shares, cumulative shares, and redeemable preference shares. Each of these shares carries a different kind of ownership and confers different kinds of rights within the company to the holder or owner of the share. This will be discussed in greater detail later in this book.

7 This means when the companies increase in value, the share price will usually go up and they will be worth more.

8 Dividends are an income similar to interest. However, interest is paid to depositors who place their money in a bank, while dividends are paid to shareholders who buy shares of a company. Deposits in a bank pay an income which depends on interest rates. It is automatic. No one needs to approve it. Dividends from shares are not automatically paid if the company makes a profit. It is the board's decision.

9 This means owners of shares have the right to sell their shares at any time during the listing period in a stock exchange in an easy way.

10 Thomas Anthony Guerriero, *How to Understand and Master Securities Laws and Regulations* (Trafford: E-Books 2012, isbn: 978-1-4669-5490-8 (e)) 78.

annual meeting.[11] Usually, the buyers of ordinary shares in particular companies will be the part-owners of those companies.[12]

### 1.1.3 Risks of Trading in Securities

Although debt equities and shares have a better financial return over the long term, they are not entirely without risk. Whilst the risk associated with government bonds is low, there have been occasions when sovereign states have defaulted on debt repayments. Corporate bonds, too, have proved to be risky investments. However, the risk associated with debt equities is generally low when compared with the stock market.

The main risk associated with buying stocks is the changing value of the shares. Share prices fluctuate daily which affects the value of the money invested. Furthermore, in the event of a company getting into financial difficulty or going bankrupt, the share price falls to zero meaning a loss of the money invested by the shareholder.

There are three main categories of risks associated with trading in shares:

1) There is no legal right to receive a dividend. The company can either distribute profits or reinvest them in their business or use them for acquisitions.[13]
2) The second risk is the economic risk arising when the share prices drop due to a change in public opinion of the company, usually connected to poor economic performance. This leads to investors selling shares which in turn drives the share price down.
3) In recent years, another type of risk has arisen known as a legal risk against the company, or a risk of legal action, which has also impacted the share price.[14]

---

11　Rodney Hobson, *Shares Made Simple: A Beginner's Guide to the Stock Market* (2nd edn, Hamman House 2012) 3.
12　It is generally accepted that the separation of ownership and control of the company is at the root of the corporate governance problem. How owners and managers interact with each other is the subject of different theories, the most popular of which is the agency theory. Agency theory describes the relation between shareholders and managers as a contractual one similar to that between a principal and an agent where the latter has a fiduciary duty to the former. However, it is debatable whether shareholders are actually owners of the company. Lynn Stout stated that shareholders own a share but the company owns itself. It is a separate legal unit and according to company law, directors owe a fiduciary duty to the company. Lynn Stout, 'Corporate Governance – What Do Shareholders Really Value?' (YouTube) <www.youtube.com/watch?v=s5Eoy988728>.
13　MacNeil (n 1) 134.
14　Ibid 24–25.

There are also risks associated with the method of buying shares. There are two ways to buy shares, namely direct or indirect purchase. When a person wants to buy shares directly, they usually do it through a traditional broker, online broker, or through a financial adviser or investment manager who will in turn go through a traditional broker.[15] Indirect buying is when people pool their money together with other people to purchase shares chosen by a professional fund manager. Indirect investment is known as a 'fund'. However, despite the risks associated with the equities and stock markets, they remain a popular avenue for investors to invest their money and grow the value of their assets.

## 1.2 Types of Securities

There are several different securities available to be bought and traded. Most legal systems categorise securities into two main types: debt and equity securities. Debt securities include corporate and sovereign bonds, while equity securities include common and preferred shares.

### 1.2.1 Debt Securities

Debt securities include corporate bonds, municipal bonds, or treasury bonds. Organisations issue debt securities to raise capital, promising interest income in exchange for the use of the money. Most debt securities pay interest at a fixed rate until the maturity date, when the principal amount is returned.

#### 1.2.1.1 Governmental and Municipal Bonds

Municipal and sovereign bonds are issued by governments to fund specific projects (such as infrastructure investment) or to fund general financial obligations. These types of bonds pay periodic interest, with the full face value being repaid on the maturity date. If a government cannot repay the face value of the bond it will default on its debt. This is referred to as a sovereign debt crisis.

In essence, bonds of this nature constitute a loan from the bondholder to the government. The government pays a fixed interest rate to the investor until the bond reaches its maturity date. Interest payments are made every six months. These kinds of investments are seen as less risky as they are backed by the government's finances. Municipal bonds represent the debt

---

15 <www.moneyadviceservice.org.uk/en/articles/investing-in-shares>.

of a provincial, territorial, municipal, or other governmental unit, other than sovereign governments.

### 1.2.1.1.1 GOVERNMENT BONDS IN THE UK

In the UK, municipal councils have recently begun to issue bonds to raise money and fund local projects. The UK Municipal Bonds Agency, set up in 2015, researched the viability of issuing municipal bonds to raise capital for local authorities. In 2020, the coronavirus pandemic led to several municipal councils in the UK issuing bonds of this kind.

### 1.2.1.1.2 GOVERNMENT BONDS IN THE US

United States federal government bonds are called Treasury bonds. The Bureau of the Fiscal Service administers the public debt by issuing and servicing US Treasury marketable savings and special securities. These bonds mature after ten years. During the ten-year period, interest is paid every six months, until maturity, at which point the owner is paid the principal amount invested. Because of their liquidity and perceived low risk, treasuries are used to manage the money supply in the open market.

### 1.2.1.1.3 GOVERNMENT BONDS IN KUWAIT

The 2014 collapse in oil prices led to several countries in the Gulf Cooperation Council (GCC) issuing sovereign bonds. Kuwait issued its first government bond in 2017 which raised US$ 8 billion. Further bonds were due to be issued in 2020 but were delayed due to the coronavirus pandemic. Government bonds in Kuwait have a five-year or ten-year maturity date.

### *1.2.1.2 Corporate Bonds and Commercial Paper*

Corporate bonds are similar in nature to government and municipal bonds. However, they are viewed as riskier as companies are generally considered to be more likely to default on debt than stable governments. Corporate bonds tend to offer higher rates of interest than government bonds, with interest usually being paid every six months. Interest rates depend on the creditworthiness of the issuing company and the duration of the bond. Longer-duration bonds pay higher interest rates as the investor is assuming greater risk.

It is important to note that bonds are not the same as commercial paper. Commercial paper describes an unsecured form of promissory note that pays a fixed rate of interest. It is typically issued by large banks to businesses to cover short-term financial obligations. Typically, these amounts are payable in one to six months of being issued, but always before the expiry of 270 days. This excludes them from the realm of regulation by the various securities laws.

In the US, corporations have various options when it comes to raising capital by means of securities. The most well known of these are:

1) *Corporate bonds*: companies issue corporate bonds to raise capital. An investor who buys a corporate bond is effectively lending money to the company in return for a series of interest payments, but these bonds may also actively trade on the secondary market.
2) *Debentures*: whilst corporate bonds are backed by the assets of the issuer, debentures are not secured by any physical assets or collateral. Debentures are issued and purchased only on the creditworthiness and reputation of the issuing party. The interest rate of bonds is generally lower than debentures. Debentures have a long maturity, typically at least ten years.
3) *Commercial paper*: this is a simple form of debt security that essentially represents a post-dated cheque with a maturity of not more than 270 days.

## 1.2.2 Equities

The terms 'equities', 'stocks', and 'shares' all refer to units of ownership in a company. The owner, known as the shareholder, has a right to a part of the company's earnings and enjoys voting rights within the company.

The weight of shareholders' votes and the number of dividends they will receive depends on the number of shares issued by a company. The minimum number of shares that can be issued by a company is one, but there is no upper limit. The total number of shares issued varies from company to company.

Table 1.1 describes the various types of shares that are issued by companies.[16]

### 1.2.2.1 Difference between Equity Security and Debt Security

An equity security is a share of equity interest in an entity such as the capital stock of a company, trust, or partnership. The most common form of equity interest is common stock, although preferred equity is also a form of capital

16 Rodney Hobson (n 11) 3–8.

*Table 1.1* Types of Shares

| Name | Definition |
|---|---|
| Ordinary shares | Each ordinary share has an equal stake in the company and one equal vote. |
| Preference shares | Investors receive a set rate of interest (similar to loans). Their dividend should be paid before ordinary shares. In the event of liquidation, preference shares should be paid off before ordinary shares. |
| Ordinary shares with additional rights | These different classes carry differing rights to vote, receive dividends, or participate in the surplus on a winding up. |
| Convertible shares | Convertible to debt in some circumstances. |
| Golden shares | Outvote all other shares put together. Used by the government when the national interest is at risk in a privatised company. |
| Vendor shares | In an acquisition matter, instead of paying cash, a company issues new shares to be given to the seller. |

stock. The holder of an equity security is a shareholder, owning a share (or fractional part) of the issuer. Equity securities generally entitle the holder to a pro-rata portion of control of the company, meaning that a holder of a majority of the equity is usually entitled to control the company (issuer).

Debt securities, on the other hand, constitute a creditor/debtor relationship, with the holder of a debt security having no ownership or voting rights in the company. Debt securities typically require regular payments of interest to the holder, with the full amount of the security being due at the end of the term.

Equity security holders do enjoy the right to profits and capital gain, whereas holders of debt securities receive only interest and repayment of the principal debt, regardless of how well the issuer performs financially. Furthermore, debt securities do not have voting rights outside of bankruptcy. It can be said that equity security holders are entitled to the 'upside' of the business and to control it.

1.2.2.1.1 EQUITIES IN THE UK

Stocks traded on the stock market in the UK are referred to as 'shares' or 'equities'. There are many different types of shares available to investors.[17] The UK securities legislation, codified into the Financial Services and Markets

---

17 Ibid 3–8.

Act 2000 (FSMA), stipulates that securities must be 'transferable',[18] which means negotiable (able to transfer from one owner to another) on a capital market. In practice, shares are traded on the London Stock Exchange. Some of the stocks traded include ordinary shares, retail bonds, and debt securities and derivatives. Other securities such as exchange-traded funds, structured products, exchange-traded commodities, covered warrants, global depository receipts, and government and municipal bonds are also traded on the Stock Exchange.[19]

### 1.2.2.1.2 EQUITIES IN THE US

In the US, the terms 'stocks' and 'shares' are used synonymously. Typically, the stock of a corporation is all of the shares into which ownership of the corporation is divided. A single share of the stock represents part ownership of the corporation in proportion to the total number of shares. This entitles the stockholder or shareholder to that part of the company's earnings and voting power at the shareholders' meeting. It should be noted that certain classes of stock may be issued; for example, without voting rights, with enhanced voting rights, or with a certain priority to receive profits or liquidation proceeds before or after other classes of shareholders.

Stock can be bought and sold privately or on stock exchanges. As new shares are issued by a company, the ownership and rights of existing shareholders are diluted in return for cash to sustain or grow the business. Companies can also buy back stock, which often lets investors recoup the initial investment plus capital gains from subsequent rises in stock price. Stock options, issued by many companies as part of employee compensation, do not represent ownership, but represent the right to buy ownership at a future time at a specified price.

---

18 Section 102(A) part 2 of the Financial Services and Markets Act 2000 (FSMA) mentions transferable securities which are defined in Article 4.1(18) of the Markets in Financial Instruments Directive (MiFID) 2004/39/EU. The MiFID directive defines transferable securities as:

'Transferable Securities' means those classes of securities which are negotiable on the capital market, with exception of payment, such as:
(a) shares in companies and other securities equivalent to shares in companies, partnership or other entities, and depositary receipts in respect of shares;
(b) bonds or other forms of securitised debt, including depositary receipts in respect of securities;
(c) any other securities giving the right to acquire or sell any such transferable securities or giving rise to a cash settlement determined by reference to transferable securities, currencies, interest rates or yields, commodities or other indices or measures.
19 <www.londonstockexchange.com/traders-and-brokers/security-types/security-types.htm>.

1.2.2.1.3 EQUITIES IN KUWAIT

The State of Kuwait has developed a complex stock market and range of financial products and services. The legal system is that of a constitutional monarchy. The laws are based on a combination of French legal traditions that have been codified into Kuwaiti law and Islamic Sharia law principles. This is important as Sharia law prohibits riba, which literally means 'increase' or interest. To make the financial markets attractive to investors (who seek to increase the value of their money), Kuwait has developed several financial systems and products that allow investors to achieve these goals.

Securities in Kuwait are regulated by the Capital Market Law of 2010. In this act, securities are defined as:

Any bond of whatever legal form that proves a share in a marketable finance licensed by authority as:

A. Shares issued or proposed to be issued in a company's capital.
B. Any instrument that originates or proves indebtedness that has been, or shall be, issued by a company.
C. Loans, bonds, and other instruments that could be convertible into shares in a company's capital.
D. All marketable general debt issued by various government entities or the public authorities and institutions.
E. The sukuk issued under the applicable Sharia-compliant contract forms.
F. Any paper or instrument considered by the Authority as a Security for the purposes of implementing this Law and the Bylaws.
G. Commercial paper, such as promissory notes, letters of credit, fund transfers, exclusively inter-bank traded instruments, insurance policies and the rights of beneficiaries on pension schemes shall not be considered as Securities.[20]

From the above definition, there are three main points that should be highlighted:

1) The definition gives the Capital Market Authority the power to decide what qualifies as securities.
2) The term 'securities' is given a broad definition in Kuwait. It includes such items as shares, loans, bonds, debt issued by government entities, *sukuk*, rights/options/derivatives, and collective investment schemes. Notably, commercial paper is excluded from the definition.

---

20 Capital Market Law 2010, Article 1. Article 1 was amended pursuant to Law No 22 of 2015 Amending Some Provisions of Law No 7 of 2010 regarding the Establishment of the Capital Markets Authority and Regulating Securities Activities.

3) The legislature has stated that commercial bills, such as cheques, bills of exchange, order notes, documentary credits, money transfers, instruments exclusively traded among banks, and insurance policies shall not be considered securities.[21]

### 1.2.2.2 Difference between Securities, Other Investments, and Commodities

There are clear differences between securities, other investments, and other commodities in which people deal.

1) The first difference is that securities (unlike goods) are not produced, but are virtually created without cost. They can be issued in unlimited amounts because securities are nothing in themselves; they symbolise only an interest in something else. Thus, securities cannot be used to acquire goods and services; they are not a kind of currency.
2) Second, securities are affected by a variety of published information.
3) In addition, many securities laws contain anti-fraud provisions since the markets for securities are uniquely at risk from deceptive practices and manipulation.
4) Furthermore, securities laws are concerned with regulation to ensure that people and firms engaged in that industry do not gain from their superior knowledge at the expense of small investors.
5) Finally, there is a range of government sanctions to punish those who break the rules and securities laws.[22]

It is apparent, therefore, that because of their nature securities need special regulation.

### 1.2.3 Derivatives/Hybrid Securities

Hybrid securities combine some of the characteristics of both debt and equity securities. Some examples of these are:

1) *Preference shares*: these shares form an intermediate class of security between equities and debt. If the issuer is liquidated, they carry the right to receive interest or a return of capital in priority to ordinary

---

21  Ibid.
22  David L Ratner and Thomas Lee Hazen, *Securities Regulation in a Nutshell* (10th edn, Thomson West 2009) 3.

shareholders. However, from a legal perspective, they are capital stock and therefore may entitle holders to some degree of control depending on whether they contain voting rights.

2) *Convertibles*: these are bonds or preferred stock that can be converted, at the election of the holder, into the common stock of the issuing company. The convertibility, however, may be forced if the convertible is a callable bond, and the issuer calls the bond. The bondholder has about one month to convert it, or the company will call the bond by giving the holder the call price, which may be less than the value of the converted stock. This is referred to as a forced conversion.

3) *Equity warrants*: these are options issued by the company that allow the holder to purchase a specific number of shares at a specified price within a specified time. They are often issued together with bonds or existing equities and are, sometimes, detachable from them and separately tradeable. When the holder of the warrant exercises it, he pays the money directly to the company, and the company issues new shares to the holder.

4) *Warrants*: like other convertible securities, these increase the number of shares outstanding, and are always accounted for in financial reports as fully diluted earnings per share, which assumes that all warrants and convertibles will be exercised.

As can be seen from the above, there are three main categories of securities that are regulated in the economies of the UK, the US, and Kuwait. There are many benefits to trading in securities as well as associated risks. For this reason, countries have developed intricate and sometimes complicated securities laws. These are discussed in Chapter 2.

# 2 Securities Law

The first chapter of this book set out a brief introduction to the various types of securities. It looked at what securities are, the benefits of securities, and the risks in trading them, as well as the various types of securities available or on offer in the UK, the US, and Kuwait. This chapter focuses on the various types of legislation surrounding securities and trading in securities in these countries.

At the outset, this chapter discusses the main aim of securities laws. In view of the wide definition of securities and the ease with which they can be traded, various laws are needed to regulate their sale or trade. These laws seek to protect both the buyer and/or investor, as well as the seller and/or issuer to ensure an orderly process. Many of these laws seek to ensure that companies accurately report their assets, financial status, and other relevant information needed by investors, but also to ensure that stockbrokers, traders, and investors abide by the rules of the trading process to stabilise the financial markets.

Securities laws can be classified according to the following categories:

1. *Transactional securities laws*: aim to regulate the purchase and sale (offer/acceptance) of securities.
2. *Regulatory securities laws*: focus on regulating the information prepared by companies that is used by investors when deciding to make an offer or purchase.
3. *Litigation securities laws*: focus on disputes between investors and companies issuing securities.
4. *Administrative securities laws*: most of these types of laws aim at alternate dispute resolution processes to avoid litigation in securities matters.

The subject of securities law differs from other fields of study such as commercial law in that it only relates to the sale and/or trade of securities,

DOI: 10.4324/9781003301875-3

whereas other laws have a wider application. In addition, company and accounting law covers listed and unlisted companies but not foreign listed companies, while securities law covers all listed companies whether foreign or national (but not unlisted national companies).

Furthermore, the methods of enforcing, supervising, and policing compliance with securities law are also different. Governmental agencies such as the UK Financial Conduct Authority (FCA), the US Securities and Exchange Commission (SEC), and the Kuwaiti Capital Markets Authority (CMA) are responsible for the enforcement and supervision of compliance with securities laws.

Despite the differences with other types of laws, securities laws do not operate in isolation from them. Most legal systems around the world are complex systems of inter-related laws that work together to form an orderly and functional society. For example, in the UK, securities laws include the Financial Services and Markets Act 2000 (FSMA) and the Financial Services Act 2012 (FSA). However, there are other laws and standards which affect securities activities, such as laws covering bribery, fraud, company law, and accounting law. In addition, financial reporting standards such as the Generally Accepted Accounting Principles (GAAP) in the UK also play a role in securities laws.

## 2.1  What Is Securities Law?

Securities law includes all laws applicable to the issuing and trading of the various securities.

After the US stock market crash in the late 1920s, governments realised the need for greater control over these trades and enacted several important pieces of legislation. Some countries, such as the UK, regulate securities as a part of the entire financial system referred to as 'financial regulation'. In other countries, such as Kuwait and the US, the regulation of securities forms part of a separate and special field of law called 'securities laws'.

Securities markets, including stock exchanges, are important for the financial system as a whole because they represent the arteries that feed the national economy with enough money to function properly.[1] There is also an overlap between the banking sector and capital markets: both have an effect on economic development, as through them savings turn into productive

---

1  'Entrance to the Capital Markets' (Qatar Financial Markets Authority) 13 <www.qfma.org .qa/App_Themes/AR/ABook/Introduction_to_capital_markets.pdf> .

investments.[2] Securities markets and the banking system complement each other, and both should be promoted to have appropriate resources for financial investments.[3] It is important to regulate the securities market because of its potential impact on the entire economy.

There is also a need for special regulation of securities because of their nature. For example, shares are intangible. The holder owns future entitlements, rights, or benefits, such as dividends, voting rights, and the return of capital, the value of which can go up or down. They are not pieces of tangible property that can be used or consumed, such as land or goods. As a result, special requirements and conditions are needed.[4] Commercial law, which encompasses the statutory regulation of commercial activities, cannot provide sufficient protection in investment markets because of the importance of having timely and full information presented in a fair way. There are also systemic risks in investment markets which bring various types of risks.[5]

There are important differences between the securities market and the traditional market for goods and services[6] as shown in Table 2.1. Because of these differences, the protection of investors requires a different approach.

*Table 2.1* Differences between Traditional and Securities Markets

| *Type of Market* | *Traditional Market* | *Securities Market* |
| --- | --- | --- |
| What is traded? | Goods and real estate | Shares, bonds, and other types |
| The necessity of the presence of intermediaries | Unnecessary | Important |
| How to implement the contract | Payment and delivery | Special method of delivery and payment |
| Physical presence of goods | Usually needed | Not needed |
| The volume of transactions | Varies | Huge, frequent, and focused |
| Announcement of prices | Do not announce prices for each deal | Official and daily announcements |

2  Elham Wahid Daham, *The Effectiveness of the Performance of Capital Markets and Banking Sector in Economic Growth* (National Centre For Legal Publications 2013) 63.

3  Mohamed Helmy Abdel Tawab, *The Legality and Technical Frames for the Stock Exchange and Mechanisms of the Legality Observation* (Dar Al Fikr Al Arabi 2012) 336.

4  Robert Baxt, Ashley Black, and Pamela Hanrahan, *Securities and Financial Services Law* (6th edn, LexisNexis 2012) 7–8.

5  MacNeil (n 1) 20.

6  Mohammed Choukri Aladawa, *Stock Exchange in the Balance of Islamic Law* (Dar Thought University 2012) 26–28.

### 2.1.1  Securities Law in the UK

The UK has a single regulatory authority that is responsible for the regulation of the whole financial system,[7] including the protection of consumers of financial products and services.[8] The UK legislation gives the Financial Conduct Authority (FCA) considerable power and broad scope.

The most important pieces of legislation regulating securities in the UK are the Financial Services and Markets Act 2000 (FSMA) and the Financial Services Act 2012 (FSA). This law is supplemented by rules and regulations set up by the Financial Conduct Authority (FCA) and set out in the FCA Handbook, namely:

1) *Listing rules*: rules related to the admission of securities to the 'Official List', which is maintained by the FCA on its website.
2) *Prospectus rules*: implement the EU Prospectus Directive in the UK and set out the content requirements for prospectuses.
3) *Disclosure and transparency rules*: implement sections of the EU Transparency Directive and make other rules concerning the transparency of and access to information in the UK financial markets including aspects of the EU Market Abuse Regulation (MAR).

### 2.1.2  Securities Law in the US

In the US, the banking system is regulated at both the federal and state level. There are separated securities, commodities, and insurance regulatory agencies – separate from the bank regulatory agencies – at the federal and state level. Banking regulations address privacy, disclosure, fraud prevention, anti-money laundering, anti-terrorism, anti-usury lending, and the promotion of lending to lower-income populations.

The Federal Reserve System is the central banking system of the United States. It was established in 1913. The three main functions of the Federal Reserve are as follows:

1. To conduct the nation's monetary policy.
2. To supervise and regulate the banking institutions.
3. To maintain the stability of the financial system and provide financial services to depository institutions, the US government, and foreign official institutions.

---

7 According to Part 1A, section 1I of the Financial Services Act 2012, the UK financial system includes 'a) financial markets and exchanges; b) regulated activities; and c) other activities connected with financial markets and exchanges'.
8 Financial Services Act 2012, part 1A, section 1B.

The Securities and Exchange Commission (SEC) is mandated with applying the various rules and laws pertaining to securities exchanges. What follows is a brief discussion of the most relevant laws and rules that the SEC needs to follow and apply.

1) *Securities Act 1933*: the Act has two basic aims:
   (i) It requires that investors receive financial and other significant information which enables them (not the government) to make informed judgements about whether to purchase a company's securities. This information includes a description of the company's properties and business, a description of the security to be offered for sale, information about the management of the company, and financial statements certified by independent accountants.
   (ii) It prohibits deceit, misrepresentations, and other fraud in the sale of securities.

2) *Securities Exchange Act 1934*:
   (i) Section (4)(a) of the Act created the Securities and Exchange Commission (SEC). The Act empowers the SEC with broad authority over all aspects of the securities industry.
   (ii) The Act requires disclosure of important information by anyone seeking to acquire more than five per cent of a company's securities by direct purchase or tender offer.
   (iii) The Act requires a variety of market participants to register with the Commission, including exchanges, brokers and dealers, transfer agents, and clearing agencies.
   (iv) According to Section 4(a), the Commission has the power to delegate any of its functions to a committee, an individual commissioner, an administrative law judge, or an employee board by publishing such order or rule.

3) *Trust Indenture Act 1939*: this Act applies to debt securities such as bonds, debentures, and notes that are offered for public sale.

4) *Investment Company Act 1940*: this Act regulates the organisation of companies, including mutual funds, that engage primarily in investing, reinvesting, and trading in securities, and whose own securities are offered to the investing public. The regulation is designed to minimise conflicts of interest that arise in these complex operations.

5) *Investment Advisers Act 1940*: this law regulates investment advisers. With certain exceptions, this Act requires that firms or sole practitioners compensated for advising others about securities investments must register with the SEC and conform to regulations designed to protect investors.

6) *Sarbanes-Oxley Act 2002*: the Act mandated a number of reforms to enhance corporate responsibility, enhance financial disclosures, and

combat corporate and accounting fraud. It created the Public Company Accounting Oversight Board (PCAOB) to oversee the activities of the auditing profession.

7) *Dodd-Frank Wall Street Reform and Consumer Protection Act 2010*: this piece of legislation set out to reshape the US regulatory system in a number of areas including but not limited to consumer protection, trading restrictions, credit ratings, regulation of financial products, corporate governance and disclosure, and transparency. The Act aims to regulate the financial industry and created programs to stop companies and lenders who took advantage of consumers prior to the financial crisis in 2008.

8) *Jumpstart Our Business Startups Act 2012*: the JOBS Act aims to help businesses raise funds in public capital markets by minimising regulatory requirements.

9) *Rules and regulations*: the SEC has the power to issue rules and regulations in respect of the work it carries out as well as to enforce compliance with these rules. Failure to comply with these rules and regulations can have serious consequences for market participants. It is generally accepted that regulation can play a significant role in the stability of the financial system.[9] This will be discussed in greater detail later in this book.

### 2.1.3  Securities Law in Kuwait

In Kuwait, securities laws were passed by the Parliament in 2010 and were amended in 2014 and 2015. These laws created the Capital Market Authority (the Authority). The Authority's responsibility to regulate financial systems is limited to securities activities, while the major responsibility for financial systems lies with the Central Bank. For example, protecting consumer loans, commissions, fees, and credit cards is the responsibility of the Central Bank. Hence, terms and conditions about the rights and obligations of consumers of financial services and products are the responsibility of the Kuwaiti Central Bank.

In the period before 2010, the Ministry of Commerce and Trade (MOCI), the Central Bank of Kuwait (CBK),[10] the Market Committee (MC), and the Kuwait Stock Exchange (KSE) were responsible for regulating and super-

---

9 Frank Partnoy, 'Financial Systems, Crises, and Regulation' (University of San Diego, Research Paper 2014 No 14–154) 2 <http://papers.ssrn.com/sol3/papers.cfm?abstract_id =2435332>.

10 The Collective Investment Scheme (CISs) was supervised by the CBK.

vising securities markets in Kuwait. The absence of a comprehensive law regulating the KSE and the lack of a single body with responsibility for its regulation resulted in some deficiencies that were exploited by unscrupulous dealers at the expense of small and large investors. There was no comprehensive and holistic legal framework, the lack of which created misunderstanding and the inability to resolve serious systemic problems.[11] In 2010, the Capital Markets Authority Act was introduced to address these problems.

The 2010 Act intended to address all previous problems by establishing a regulatory authority that was responsible for overseeing securities activities. In addition, several illegal activities related to securities were banned for the first time, such as insider dealing, manipulation, and misleading the market. The new Kuwaiti securities law annulled all previous securities legislation or any legislation contradicting its provisions. Article 163 states that:

Firstly: Following the end of the provisional phases referred to in this Law, the following laws, decrees-laws and decrees shall be annulled:

1. Decree issued on 14 August 1983 regulating Kuwait Stock Exchange Market.
2. Decree regulating the settlement of securities trading and the clearing room at Kuwait Stock Exchange dated 27 December 1986.
3. Law No 12 of 1998 concerning Licensing the Establishment of Leasing and Investment Companies.
4. Decree-Law No 31 of 1990 on Regulating the Trading of Securities and Establishment of Investment Funds.
5. Law No 2 of 1999 concerning Declaration (disclosure) of Interests in Shareholding Companies' Shares.

Secondly: Provisions of Articles (from 323 to 328) of the Commerce Law shall not apply to Exchanges to which the provisions of this Law apply.

Thirdly: Provisions of Chapter (5) and Chapter (6) of Section (9) of the Companies Law shall be cancelled.

---

11 Khaled Helmy, *Legal Regulation of the Securities Market in Egyptian and Kuwaiti Law: With the Study of the Impact of the Global Financial Crisis on Arab Capital Markets* (University of Kuwait 2010) 170.

The second chapter of the Act deals with the Capital Market Authority (CMA) and its objectives, duties, powers, and managing the Board's authority. According to the Act, the CMA's objectives are:

1. Regulate securities activities in a fair, transparent, and efficient manner.
2. Grow the capital markets and diversify and develop investment instruments thereof in accordance with best international practice.
3. Enhance investors' protection.
4. Reduce systemic risks arising from securities activities.
5. Impose requirements of full disclosure to achieve fairness and transparency, and to prevent conflicts of interests and the use of insider information.
6. Enhance compliance with the rules and regulations related to securities activities.
7. Enhance public awareness of securities activities and of the benefits, risks, and obligations arising from investments in securities and encourage their development.

The Act was the first major attempt at addressing the issues of trading in securities in Kuwait. An amendment to this law was passed in 2015 that attempted to expand the scope of the legislation. However, there are still many areas in which the legal framework of securities law in Kuwait can be improved.

The Explanatory Memorandum to the 2015 amendment stated that the 2010 law that created the CMA and regulated securities activities aimed to respond to the progress in the domain of financial activities. However, after several years it had become necessary to amend some provisions of the law to become compatible with the dictates of work and progress. Hence, the resulting amendments aim to keep abreast of the successive progress in this vital economic and financial activity sector.[12]

## 2.2  Financial Regulation

Financial regulation refers to rules and laws enacted for the regulation and supervision of all businesses and institutions in the financial industry. Institutions such as banks, credit unions, insurance companies, financial brokers, and asset managers are subject to certain requirements, restrictions, and guidelines, aimed at maintaining the stability and integrity of the financial system. Financial regulation can be the task of governments

---

12  < www.cma.gov.kw/ar/web/cma/cma-handbook>.

and governmental organisations, or it can be managed by independent organisations. The various institutions that are tasked with oversight ensure that the rules and laws are complied with.

### 2.2.1 Why Is Financial Regulation Necessary?

The objectives of financial regulation are:

1) Market confidence: to maintain confidence in the financial system.
2) Financial stability: contributing to the protection and enhancement of stability of the financial system.
3) Consumer protection: securing the appropriate degree of protection for consumers.

Poorly regulated financial institutions have the potential to undermine the stability of the financial system, harm consumers, and can damage the prospects for the economy. Financial regulation aims to put rules in place to prevent this and to safeguard the wider financial system and protect consumers.

### 2.2.2 Enforcement and Resolution

Having rules and laws, and making sure financial services providers follow them, are the first two elements to understanding financial regulation. Enforcement and resolution are the third. Where a firm is found in breach of the rules, several steps can be taken. In serious cases, this can lead to the firm facing enforcement proceedings. Having the credible threat of enforcement is essential to deter poor behaviour in the financial services sector. Finally, there are times when resolution is the only outcome. Resolution is the process of winding down or restructuring a financial institution in a way that minimises harm to the economy.

### 2.2.3 Financial Markets and Theories of Financial Regulation

In general, financial markets refer to the meeting place of one party with money to invest and another party with an idea that can be invested in.[13] There are two ways of looking at finance. The first is to focus on the theory of finance, which views financial economics as a scientific discipline. The

---

13 Mokhtar Hamida, *Privatisation Through The Financial Markets* (Hassan Modern Library 2013) 87.

second is about solving problems in practice.[14] However, there is no clear scientific solution to these problems.

American economist and author, Robert Shiller, said that financial markets are not just about trading. Financial markets include banking, insurance, securities, future markets, and the derivatives market.[15] There are four main types of financial services, namely, banking, securities, insurance, and non-bank credit.[16] Shiller divided financial market regulation into five types.

1) *Internal regulation*: when a company sets its own rules, these are called internal rules. The board, including internal and external directors, imposes certain principles. Members of a board owe two important duties to the firm. First, they owe a duty of care; namely, they should have sufficient knowledge and expertise related to their role in the company, which includes acting as a reasonable person who obtains information, monitors all developments that could impact the company, and is careful about their obligations as a member of the board. The second is that of loyalty, not simply to the shareholders, but also to the firm. There is a growing belief that loyalty should be extended to stakeholders, other people, and the community.

2) *Self-regulation*: the second type of regulation refers to trade groups or 'self-regulation'. This happens when groups of firms or people decide to pass rules among themselves to form an organisation. Self-regulation occurs when regulations are specified, administered, and enforced by the organisation itself.[17] Self-regulatory organisations (SROs) should be subject to the oversight of a regulatory authority.[18] Shiller cited the New York Stock Exchange as an example of a trade group. As there was no organised stock exchange, in 1792 stockbrokers signed an agreement setting up the Stock Exchange to regulate the prices and the commissions. Twenty-four stockbrokers gathered under a buttonwood tree outside the building located at 68 Wall Street to sign what became known as the 'Buttonwood Agreement'. This agreement remained until 1974 when

---

14  Nico Van Der Wijst, *Finance: A Quantitative Introduction* (Cambridge University Press 2013) 2.

15  Robert Shiller, 'Financial Market 2011' (Open Yale University courses).

16  'Good Practices for Financial Consumer Protection' (2012) World Bank working paper 5.

17  Ian Bartte and Peter Vass, 'Self-Regulation and the Regulatory State: a Survey of Policy and Practice' (University of Bath, Research Report 17) 22.
    <www.bath.ac.uk/management/cri/pubpdf/Research_Reports/17_Bartle_Vass.pdf>.

18  IOSCO Objectives and Principles of Securities Regulation (2010) Principle 9 <www.iosco .org/library/pubdocs/pdf/IOSCOPD323.pdf>.

the government broke the monopoly. Over time, Wall Street has come to represent the financial markets of the United States as a whole.[19]

3) *Local regulation*: the third type of regulation is local regulation. For example, the American Blue-Sky Laws are financial regulations issued by each state. The first was issued in 1911 in Kansas, and almost every state had its own law until the 1930s.

4) *National regulation*: to complete the previous example, after 1934, all listed companies in the United States were regulated by the Securities and Exchange Commission (SEC).

5) *International regulation*: there are several international organisations, such as the International Monetary Fund (IMF),[20] the Bank of International Settlements (BIS),[21] and the Basel Committee on Banking Supervision (BCBS).[22] One problem with national regulations is that people may leave the country if they do not like the regulations. Therefore, attempts to have international regulations include:

(i) The BIS in Basel, created in 1930. It includes 57 central banks and suggests rules that have a real effect even though they are not enforceable by law.

(ii) The Basel Committee of 1974, which suggested bank regulations and was followed by Basel 1 in 1988, Basel 2 in 2004, and Basel 3 in 2010.

(iii) The G6, which comprised six major countries: France, Germany, Italy, Japan, the US, and the UK. In 1976, Canada was added, and the group became the G7. In 2008, the group was extended to be the G20 to represent the leading financial countries in the rest of the world. In 2009, the G20 created the Financial Stability Board (FSB) located in Basel to report recommendations to the G20 about the world's financial systems.

---

19 <www.nyx.com/en/who-we-are/history/new-york>.

20 187 countries are members of the IMF. It has a number of objectives and functions, such as maintaining financial stability by developing international cooperation, encouraging international trade, reducing global poverty, encouraging high levels of employment, and providing loans. In addition, it monitors, advises, educates, and trains the financial and economic police for its 187 member countries; Nicholas Ryder, Margaret Griffiths, and Lachmi Singh, *Commercial Law: Principles And Policy* (CUP 2012) 464.

21 It supports central banks to maintain monetary and financial stability. It has a number of objectives and functions, such as promoting discussion among central banks; ibid 465.

22 It has a number of objectives and functions, such as improving awareness and enhancing the levels of banking supervision; ibid.

## 2.3  Prudential Regulation vs Conduct of Business Regulation

National financial market regulation can be divided into two categories, namely prudential regulation and the conduct of business regulation.

1) Prudential regulation is about controlling the solvency and liquidity of participants in financial markets.[23]
2) Conduct of business regulation focuses on the relationship between firms and customers, such as disclosure rules.[24] It includes preventing market abuse and ensuring that firms treat consumers fairly.[25]

Prudential regulation can be separated into macro-prudential regulation and micro-prudential regulation.[26] The latter is about ensuring that the solvency of individual financial firms is not compromised by excessive risk-taking or other questionable practices, while the former is about protecting the stability of the financial system as a whole.[27] Micro-prudential regulation includes promulgating principles that firms must observe to ensure that they conduct their business in a prudent matter.[28] For example, in the UK, the macro-prudential function is carried out by the Financial Policy Committee (FPC). The responsibility for micro-prudential regulation is divided between the FCA and the Prudential Regulation Authority (PRA). The latter is responsible for banks, large deposit-takers, and others, the failure of which can impact the system. Some 1,400 financial groups are supervised by the PRA, while approximately 23,000 firms are supervised by the FCA.[29]

The question here is how to properly regulate the financial system. For example, in the UK before and during the 2008 financial crisis there was a conflict between prudential supervision and the conduct of business supervision. It was difficult for one body to reconcile these issues. The former is largely an economic activity, while the latter is often performed by lawyers. A tripartite committee, which was responsible for financial stability in the UK and included the Treasury, the Bank of England, and the FSA, was not

---

23  MacNeil (n 1) 36.
24  Ibid 37.
25  Emma Murphy and Stephen Senior, 'Changes to the Bank of England' (2013) 20 <www .bankofengland.co.uk/publications/Documents/quarterlybulletin/2013/qb130102.pdf>.
26  This distinction between regulations first occurred in 2000, while in the past there was a mixture between them. Robert Shiller (n 37).
27  Iain G MacNeil (n 1) 36.
28  Emma Murphy and Stephen Senior (n 47) 20.
29  Ibid.

able to limit that conflict. The FSA focused too much on the conduct of business at the expense of micro-prudential supervision.[30] To reduce the conflict, there is a new approach that gives the Bank of England responsibility for micro-prudential supervision (shadow banking sector), which means that it oversees some individual firms in addition to macro-prudential supervision (financial stability of the economy) and its monetary policy role.[31] Kuwait and the US have a different approach towards financial regulation of the financial sector.

---

30  <www.publications.parliament.uk/pa/ld200809/ldselect/ldeconaf/101/10108.htm>.
31  Ibid.

# 3  Laws Related to Securities

This chapter discusses other laws that are related to securities. These include fraud and bribery laws, accounting laws, and company law. In this regard, a brief discussion of the legal systems used in the different countries is set out to show how securities laws form part of the broader legal framework. This section focuses on other areas of legislation that are in some way related to securities laws.

## 3.1  Legal Systems

Each country has its own legal system that has developed over time to suit its needs. In each of these legal systems, securities laws have developed along with a framework of legal requirements and other related laws. A multi-faceted interplay of economic, social, and political factors has affected the current legal systems in the UK, the US, and Kuwait.

### 3.1.1  Legal System of the UK

The UK legal system is known as a common law system. This type of system combines both legislation passed by Parliament as well as the creation of various precedents by courts. The sources of English law are case law, Acts of Parliament, statutory interpretations, delegated legislation, European law, custom, equity, and treaties. The decisions made by judges in cases brought before them are termed case law. As a result, judges are empowered to make legal findings that have the effects of laws.

The advantages of case law are:

  i. Certainty.
 ii. All the cases are treated equally.
iii. Detailed practical rules.

DOI: 10.4324/9781003301875-4

Whilst statutes are based on theory and logic, they do not always address every conceivable situation. As a result, cases will appear before courts that require judges to interpret the law in line with real situations as set out in the facts of each matter. By making legal findings and interpreting the statutes, the laws are expanded and their influence increased. This is especially important when considering that a changing society needs laws that are flexible and open to interpretation. This flexibility allows for laws to be developed along certain lines that address the needs of society.

On the other hand, there are disadvantages to the approach of case law. First, due to the sheer volume of cases being tried, and the complexity of these cases, thousands of law reports are produced. Hence, it may be difficult to understand case law and keep up to date with any changes that are made. It can also make case law rather rigid because sometimes judges disagree with a law's interpretation but are bound to follow the precedent set by higher courts.

A second negative aspect of case law is that judges sometimes make illogical distinctions based on the facts of the case. This creates uncertainty and unpredictability in differing circumstances. Since judges are not elected officials, it could be argued that the power conferred upon them to make legal precedent is not justified in modern democracies.

In UK law, the statutes (Acts of Parliament) are sovereign; that is, they take precedence over case law. The UK constitutional law comprises Acts of Parliament (statute), common law (judicial decisions), and conventions (long-established traditions about the right way to behave).[1]

### 3.1.2 Legal System of the US

In the US, the legal system is based on several fundamental principles set out in the following.

1) *States vs federal law*: the US is made up of 50 different states, each with its own laws and regulations. Whilst there is a great deal of similarity between laws in different states, each state has its own legislature that is entitled to make laws that apply in that area. State law is applicable only in that state. However, federal law is applicable in every state in the country. Whilst state laws may differ, federal law is consistent.

---

1 Catherine Elliott and Frances Quinn, *English Legal System* (12th edn, Pearson 2011) 2.

2) *Court hierarchy*: the courts are structured into three tiers of hierarchy.
   (i) The first tier in the federal court systems is the District Courts (94 district courts). This is usually a court of first instance when dealing with matters related to federal law.
   (ii) Once matters have been heard in the District Court, appeals may be made to the second tier in the federal court process, namely to Courts of Appeal (13 circuits).
   (iii) The highest and most important court in the country is the Supreme Court. There is only one Supreme Court and once matters have been finalised in this court there is no further appeals process available. The Supreme Court usually deals with matters relating to federal law and constitutional law as well as appeals from lower courts.
3) *Dual court systems*: all states have their own court systems in conjunction with the federal courts and the Supreme Court.
4) *Jurisdiction*: the term jurisdiction refers to the formal power of a court to exercise authority over a particular matter. It is further defined as the authority of the court to hear the particular type of matter as well as the geographic region or area of jurisdiction. For example, lower courts do not have the jurisdiction or authority to hear matters relating to federal law. Furthermore, courts in Los Angeles do not have the jurisdiction to hear matters that occurred in New York (or any other jurisdiction other than Los Angeles).
5) *Precedent*: the term precedent refers to the principle whereby lower courts are compelled to follow the decisions made by higher courts. All lower courts are compelled to follow the decisions of the Supreme Court. Courts of equal division (such as state courts) are not compelled to follow the decisions of other such courts; for example, a Los Angeles state court is not obliged to follow the decisions of the New York state courts.
6) *Mandatory/binding versus persuasive authority*: the principle of precedent requires that courts enforce the decisions of higher courts in similar matters. However, not all precedent is binding on lower courts. In certain circumstances, precedent can be seen as persuasive rather than mandatory or binding.
7) *Primary versus secondary authority*: primary legal sources are the actual law in the form of the Constitution, federal and state statutes, court cases (precedent), and administrative rules and regulations. Secondary legal sources may restate the law, but they also discuss, analyse, describe, explain, or critique it as well.

### 3.1.3 Legal System of Kuwait

In Kuwait, Islamic law is considered sacred. The main sources of Sharia Islamic law are the Quran, the Sunnah (the prophet's traditions), the Ijma (consensus of Muslim jurists), and the Qiyas (judgment upon juristic analogy). Sharia Islamic law has widespread application in the Arabian Peninsula.

The largest economic event in the history of Kuwait was the discovery of oil and natural gas in the region. Previously, the main economic activities were agriculture, fishing, trade, and pearl-diving[2] in addition to camel and sheep herding. The discovery of oil created a new economic, social, and political order which could no longer rely solely on customs and Sharia Islamic law. Consequently, Kuwait decided to adopt the Egyptian-French model[3] as a basis for its national legal system.

In 1960, Kuwait adopted its constitution, forming a basis for a new legal system. Article 2 of the Kuwaiti Constitution provides that, 'The religion of the state is Islam and Islamic Shari'ah is a principal source for legislation'.[4] This means that Sharia is not the *exclusive* source of Kuwaiti law, as it also includes many codes, such as civil, commercial, company, and criminal codes. However, Sharia law still plays an integral part in the legal system. For example, in civil cases, if a situation is not included in the code, the judge must consider Sharia law.[5]

In Kuwait, there are clear distinctions between the three branches of authority, namely, the legislature, executive, and judiciary. Article 50 of the Kuwaiti Constitution states that the system of government is based on the principle of separation of powers, functioning in co-operation with each other in accordance with the provisions of the Constitution. The Kuwaiti judicial system[6] is comprised of three stages of adjudication. All courts in Kuwait pass sentences in the name of the Emir. Article 53 of the Kuwaiti Constitution says that the judicial power is vested in the courts, which exercise it in the name of the Emir within the limits of the Constitution.

The Securities Law of 2010 created a new court of first instance, and appeal, as well as established a special[7] prosecution body. In terms of

---

2  Ahmed Al-Suwaidi, *Finance of International Trade in the Gulf* (Graham & Trotman 1994) 9.

3  The French legal system spread into some Arab countries through Egypt.

4  Ahmed Al-Suwaidi (n 55) 25.

5  Article 1 Kuwaiti Civil Law, amended in 1996.

6  In Kuwait, there are different levels of courts, namely summary, first instance, appeals, and cassation courts. The latter considers solely the law without looking at the facts.

7  Article 164 mentions that 'This Law shall be considered a special law and its provisions shall be considered special provisions. All provisions contained in any general or special laws inconsistent with the provisions hereof are hereby cancelled'. According to Kuwaiti legal system the judges must follow the securities law.

this law, a new Capital Markets Court[8] was established. Its purpose was to decide penal cases relating to the securities laws and also to decide non-penal cases relating to commercial, civil, and administrative matters emanating from the Act. In addition, a special prosecution body called the Capital Market Prosecution[9] was established with the purpose of investigating and prosecuting crimes falling within the jurisdiction of the Capital Markets Court. To date, this court has not had a tremendous impact on the securities market and regulation thereof. However, it has been instrumental in training judges and prosecutors in various matters relating to the trade in securities.

## 3.2  Fraud and Bribery Laws

When discussing securities laws, it is customary to include details of fraud and bribery legislation in various countries. These laws may be designed for different circumstances but have specific applications in the securities field. They are especially important when dealing with the protection of investors and the sale of securities on the stock market.

### 3.2.1  Fraud and Bribery Laws in the UK

The crime of corporate fraud is defined in the Fraud Act 2006 (UK). It states that:

> A person by their action, or lack of action, may be found guilty of fraud if they breach or commit any of following:
>
> - Fraud by false representation.[10]
> - Fraud by failing to disclose information.[11]
> - Fraud by abuse of position.[12]

Bribery is an example of an offence which can harm securities activities. However, it is not covered by securities legislation but by the Bribery Act 2010 in the UK. The risk of bribery applies to all companies, large and small, and it needs to be countered because it harms securities activities. Receiving and offering bribes can damage society and economic growth.

---

8  Article 108.
9  Article 114.
10  Fraud Act 2006 s2.
11  Fraud Act 2006 s3.
12  Fraud Act 2006 s4.

Bribery damages competition and free markets and rewards unethical behaviour.[13]

Bribery can harm securities activities in one of two ways. The company which pays the bribe is depressing its profit, which affects its shareholders. There can also be an adverse effect on the shareholders of a competing firm, which may have lost out because of the unfair advantage created by the bribing action of its competitor. On the other hand, some could argue that without bribery the company would not get business, especially with overseas countries.

A good example of this is Hewlett-Packard (HP). The company bribed public officials in Poland, Russia, and Mexico to gain public contracts.[14] In the UK, the Bribery Act 2010 was passed to create some new offences that apply to all companies that do business in the UK. The former Secretary of State for Justice in the UK, Kenneth Clarke, supported this idea in the Foreword to the Guidance of the Bribery Act 2010, saying 'we do not have to decide between tackling corruption and supporting growth'.[15]

In the UK, section 6 of the Act addresses the offence of bribing foreign public officials. This is different from the general bribery offences set out under section 1, relating to bribing another person, and under section 2 relating to the person being bribed. The two offences of bribing and being bribed replace the common law offences and the Acts of 1889, 1906, and 1916.[16]

Under section 6, a person commits a crime if they bribe a foreign public official on the condition that the bribe is intended to influence the capacity of the foreign public official. Part (2) of section 6 mentions that the bribery must have the intention to obtain or to keep hold of business or an advantage in conducting business. According to section 6, part (3b), the only exemption is if there is an applicable written law that allows influence by such things (offer, promise, or gift). However, there is no country in the world that allows its officials to be bribed, so this exemption is of no value.

Section 7 of the Bribery Act (UK) refers to a commercial organisation which could be guilty of an offence if a person associated with it, who

---

13 <www.theguardian.com/sustainable-business/blog/eliminating-corruption-crucial
   -sustainablity>.
14 Ibid.
15 The Bribery Act 2010, Guidance <www.justice.gov.uk/downloads/legislation/bribery-act
   -2010-guidance.pdf>.
16 Stephen Bloomfield, *Theory and Practice Corporate Governance: An Integrated Approach*
   (Cambridge University Press 2013) 113.

performs services for the commercial organisation or on its behalf, such as an employee, agent, or subsidiary, uses bribery to obtain or retain business or secure an advantage in the conduct of business. However, it is a defence for the company to prove that it had in place adequate procedures to prevent such things. The Act treats a company as a separate body, which has its own entity and its own responsibilities.[17] Any fine against the company could affect innocent shareholders. However, some argue that the shareholders must be more careful when electing the board to ensure that they will not be susceptible to bribery.[18]

The penalties for individuals include imprisonment for up to ten years and an unlimited fine for the company. In the UK, the first conviction under the Bribery Act was on 5 December 2014 against a former Director and Chief Commercial Officer of Sustainable AgroEnergy plc (SAE), Gary West, who was convicted of being bribed under s2 of the Bribery Act. The second person, Stuart Stone, who was convicted under s1 of the Bribery Act of offering or giving bribes, was a sales agent of unregulated pension and investment products for a separate company. West received bribes from Stone.[19]

### 3.2.2 Fraud and Bribery Laws in the US

The legal approach to combating bribery in the US is more complex than that in the UK. Whilst the UK legislators have codified the legal framework dealing with bribery into one or two pieces of legislation, in the US there are different laws and regulations at both state and federal levels that apply in different circumstances. As previously mentioned, the American legal system is divided into federal and state legal systems and both are involved in combatting bribery. Both systems share enforcement power in circumstances where bribery has taken place.

In the US, combating bribery can be divided into three categories:

1) Bribing (or attempting to bribe) a public official.
2) Bribery between private individuals or companies.
3) Bribing of a foreign public official.

---

17 John Rupp, 'The UK Bribery Act 2010 and Its Implications for Businesses: Corporate Governance for Main Market and AIM Companies' (White Paper, London Stock Exchange 2012) 115.

18 Stephen Bloomfield (n 71) 112.

19 <www.corderycompliance.com/23-million-bribery-case-leads-to-28-years-in-jail/>.

At the federal level, there are two important statutes dealing with bribery including the Foreign Corrupt Practices Act 1977 (FCPA) and the Federal Bribery Statute. Federal law criminalises bribery of domestic as well as foreign public officials.

### 3.2.2.1  Foreign Corrupt Practices Act 1977 – Corruption of Foreign Public Officials

The Foreign Corrupt Practices Act 1977 (FCPA) was enacted to combat the bribery of foreign public officials in international business transactions. One of the most famous cases falling within the scope of this section relates to the situation where corporations contributing to the re-election of President Nixon paid bribes to high officials of foreign governments.

The main purpose of the FCPA is to ban companies and their individual officers from affecting foreign officials with any payments or rewards. The Act aims to prevent US individuals and companies from being involved in corruption of foreign officials abroad. However, US individuals and companies have realised that corruption is a part of doing business in certain parts of the world. For this reason, US law enforcement agencies try to ensure that these types of actions do not become common practice. As a result, it is suggested that countries around the world adopt similar legislation banning all forms of corruption of foreign public officials and businesses to ensure a 'level playing field'.

The Securities and Exchange Commission (SEC) and the Department of Justice (DOJ) can enforce the FCPA. The bribery sections provide for civil and criminal enforcement by the Justice Department. The DOJ is the primary prosecutorial body with the power to prosecute corruption on the federal level in the United States. The SEC enforces the Act for companies it regulates.

The anti-bribery provisions of the FCPA apply to any issuer of securities, any company required to register its securities with the SEC, or any officer, director, employee, agent, or stockholder acting on behalf of such issuer, any 'domestic concern' or any officer, director, employee, or agent thereof or any stockholder acting on behalf of such domestic concern or any person other than an issuer or domestic concern or any officer, director, employee, or agent or shareholder.

### 3.2.2.2  Federal Bribery Statute – Domestic Bribery of US Public Officials

The Federal Bribery Statute is the most important statute that most directly criminalises federal public corruption involving public officials.

Section 201 (a)(1) forbids bribes and gratuities given or offered to or received or requested by a public official. The term 'public official' is defined to include any:

> Member of Congress, Delegate, or Resident Commissioner, either before or after such official has qualified, or an officer or employee or person acting for or on behalf of the United States, or any department, agency or branch of Government thereof, including the District of Columbia, in any official function, under or by authority of any such department, agency, or branch of Government, or a juror.[20]

Section 201(b) criminalises the giving and receiving of bribes. As to the giver, § 201(b) requires the prosecution to show that something of value was corruptly given, offered, or promised, directly or indirectly, to a public official. Section 201(c) deals with illegal official 'gratuity'. Section 201(c) defines a gratuity as something of value that was given, offered, or promised to a public official with the intention of getting the official to perform something in return for the gratuity. The clause includes a provision that states that the gratuity or something of value should have been demanded, sought, received, accepted, or agreed to by the official.

In terms of the Act, the punishment for bribing an official is punishable by up to 15 years' imprisonment, a fine of US$ 250,000 (US$ 500,000 for organisations) or up to three times the value of the bribe, whichever is greater, and disqualification from holding any federal office.

Both the US DOJ and SEC are authorised to punish domestic bribery, which can be defined as bribery of an individual or commercial entity (private to private). This is punishable as a felony under state law and carries the penalty as stipulated by the specific state legislation. However, only 36 states have laws specifically prohibiting commercial bribery. State and local prosecutors can bring criminal charges for violations of state anti-corruption laws.

The SEC has broad authority to address civil violations of the FCPA involving publicly listed companies. The SEC can prosecute cases of domestic bribes that violate the SEC's activities. They are able to pursue the matter in civil courts or refer the matter to the DOJ for criminal prosecution.

---

20  18 USC § 201(a)(1).

### *3.2.3 Fraud and Bribery Laws in Kuwait*

In Kuwait, for a criminal offence to be committed a bribe must be given to a government official in Kuwait.[21] Article 35 of Kuwaiti Criminal Law of 1960 mentions that bribery occurs if a public officer 'government employee' requests or obtains something (money, gifts, or any types of interests) in consideration of the fulfilment of his duty. Article 43 states that any employee working in a company in which the government has a share is deemed to be a public official for the purposes of the Kuwaiti bribery legislation. In effect, Kuwait has limited the protection to listed companies if the Kuwaiti government owns part of the shares.

In an attempt to address some of these issues and to fight corruption and fraud, Kuwait introduced a new body in 2016 called the Kuwait Anticorruption Authority. Article 4 of the Kuwait Anticorruption Authority (Nazaha) establishment law identifies its goals as the following:

- To work on the fight against corruption, prevent its risks and effects, prosecute its perpetrators, confiscate, and recover funds and proceeds resulted from the practice thereof in accordance with the law.
- To protect State bodies from bribery, trading in influence and abuse of power for personal benefits and prevent mediation and nepotism.

## 3.3 Company Law

Securities law and company or corporate law are two separate fields of study. However, many of their provisions overlap. In brief, securities laws require companies to disclose certain information that is used by investors. Company law seeks to regulate the operation of the company, focusing on its internal affairs and corporate governance issues. This is of value to investors as companies that are compliant with company law are seen as good and/or safe investment opportunities.

Shareholders of securities are affected by company law, but it is limited to certain actions, such as the right to approve important decisions (e.g., amending the Articles of Association) and electing or removing directors.[22] In the UK, there are some rights available under company law to protect

---

21 Kuwaiti Criminal Law.
22 Henry R Cheeseman, *Business Law: Legal Environment, Online Commerce, Business Ethics, and International Issues* (8th edn, Pearson 2013) 618.

minority shareholders;[23] for example, any shareholder can demand a copy of the company's last annual reporting statements.[24] Furthermore, a shareholder can approach the court due to unfair prejudice to the shareholder.[25] If the court agrees it may compensate the shareholder or regulate future conduct of the company. Examples of prejudicial conduct are mismanagement, the majority taking financial advantage of minority shareholders, exclusion from management, non-payment of dividends or reducing dividends by paying excessive remuneration, and improper allotments.[26]

Some people feel that company law should go further to protect securities owners from board actions which may adversely affect the company's share price and even jeopardise its survival. For example, a board member could take money from the company, or take advantage of their position by selling a company's assets to relatives at a low price or buying at a high price to favour someone, pay a favoured employee a high salary, or deal as an insider. Minority shareholders need to protect their investment against the majority who have the power to influence the board of directors.

### 3.3.1  Company Law in the UK

Company law in the UK has been codified into the Companies Act 2006. Together with additional or secondary laws, this Act has created a regime with which companies in the UK must comply. The requirements are far-reaching and contain several sanctions such as financial penalties, disqualification of directors, and personal liability for debts incurred by the company. In essence, the Companies Act 2006 regulates how companies operate, how investors are involved in the day-to-day running of the company, the issuing of shares, and the preparation of financial reports.

### 3.3.2  Company Law in the US

In the US, in addition to federal securities laws, which create minimum standards for trade in company shares and governance rights, each state has

---

23  Majority and minority shareholders can be described as controlling and non-controlling shareholders respectively; Paul Davies, *Introduction to Company Law* (2nd edn, Oxford University Press 2010) 218–219.

24  'Protection For Minority Shareholders' (2014) Institute of Directors working paper 3.

25  Company Act 2006 s994.

26  Natasa Flourentzou, 'Minority Shareholders: Applicability of Unfair Prejudice' (MS Lawyers)
    <www.mslawyers.eu/images/publication_documents/Minority_Shareholders-_Applicability_of_Unfair_Prejudice.pdf>.

its own basic company law. According to the US Constitution and decisions of the Supreme Court, companies are entitled to register in any state that they choose. In this regard, it is interesting to note that most larger corporations prefer to be registered in the state of Delaware even though they operate nationally and may have little or no business in Delaware itself. This is because Delaware offers lower corporate taxes, fewer shareholder rights against directors, and has developed a specialised court and legal profession.

To establish a company, the founders are required to prepare a set of articles or charter which outlines the name and purpose of the business. The charter records the corporation's name, purposes or duration, identifies whether all shares will have the same rights, and gives other details about the company. Furthermore, bylaws are required to set out the rights and obligations of management as well as the number of directors, the arrangement of the board, requirements for corporate meetings, duties of office-holders, etc.

To attract major corporations to register in their state, many state legislatures have tried to limit the amount of legislation and regulations relating to company law. This led to the so-called 'race to the bottom' where each state legislator tried to do whatever it could to attract corporations to their state. This problem was increasingly thought to justify federal regulation of corporations because each state tried to attract companies to incorporate under its law.

A good example of federal laws that were passed to address this situation is the Dodd-Frank Act of 2010. To illustrate the relationship between federal and state laws, shareholders in Delaware companies can make appointments to the board through a majority vote and can also act to expand the size of the board and elect new directors with a majority. However, directors themselves will often control which candidates can be nominated or appointed to the board. Different states tried to lure corporations to their state by passing state laws that gave the board of directors more control over the process of nominations and appointments to the board. This in part led to shareholders' rights being limited or encroached upon. For this reason, a federal law, the Dodd-Frank law,[27] was passed to empower the SEC[28] to write regulations that curtailed the power of boards of directors (granted by state law) and would allow shareholders to propose nominations to the board. However, companies took the matter to court in

---

27 §971.
28 SEC Rule 14a-11.

order to limit the effect of these laws. In the case of *In Business Roundtable v SEC*[29] they succeeded in limiting the effect of the federal law and have been able to create a monopoly on nominating future directors. This serves to illustrate that there is an ongoing battle between federal and state law, as well as the courts, in defining and interpreting company law.

### 3.3.3  Company Law in Kuwait

Company law in Kuwait was first regulated by the introduction of Law Number 25 of 2012 (the Companies Law) which aimed to replace Law No 15 of 1960. This law set out to deal with matters such as non-profit companies, holding companies, and shareholders' agreements. However, this law has been amended several times in line with practical considerations, the most recent of which was passed in 2016.[30]

The 2016 Companies Law expanded the forms of companies that may be registered in Kuwait. Hence, it provides for more types of companies that can be established in Kuwait, such as the incorporation of non-profit companies, which are now permissible under the Companies Law in order to undertake a social role. Moreover, new forms of companies have been introduced, such as a sole person company and professional companies. Professional companies may take the form of a closed shareholding company, limited partnership, or a company with limited liability.

Further, the 2016 Companies Law also has changed some provisions with respect to holding companies. Holding companies may take the form of a closed shareholding company, a limited liability company, or a sole person company.

With respect to the incorporation procedures of companies, it is acknowledged that the process for starting a business in Kuwait is lengthy and complicated thereby hindering commerce and the establishment of new companies. To address this issue, the Companies Law has adopted what is known as the 'one window system' for finalising the procedures of incorporating companies. These are now completed through a special department for this purpose at the Ministry of Commerce and Industry, which comprises representatives of the concerned government bodies to ensure prompt finalisation of the incorporation procedures. The aim of the Companies Law is to facilitate the entire process, while encouraging more investors to establish companies in Kuwait.

---

29  905 F 2d 406 (DC Cir 1990).
30  Law No 1 of 2016.

The forms of companies that are commonly registered are:

- General partnership company.
- Limited partnership company.
- Partnership limited by shares.
- Joint venture company.
- Closed shareholding company.
- Public shareholding company.
- Limited liability company.
- Single person company.
- Professional company.
- Holding company.

The relationship between company law and securities law is particularly important when dealing with public shareholding companies. These companies are established in terms of companies laws but are regulated in terms of securities laws once they list on the stock exchange.

Article 119 of the Companies Law defines a Public Shareholding Company as:

> A company whose capital is divided into tradable shares of equal value in the manner prescribed in this law. The responsibility of the shareholder shall be limited to the contribution of the value of the shares subscribed for by him and he shall not be liable for the company's obligations, except to the extent of the nominal value of the shares in which he has subscribed.

Furthermore, Article 128 mentions that:

> The invitation of the public to subscribe in the company's shares shall be made according to a subscription prospectus that includes the particulars and procedures stipulated in Law No (7) of 2010 and its executive regulations.

To create a public shareholding company, the approval of the Supervisory Authorities is needed. In this regard, Article 6 of the 2016 Companies Law mentions that:

> The approval of the Central Bank of Kuwait or the Capital Market Authority, as applicable, is required with regard to the incorporation of companies and to the Company Contract, which are subject to the supervision of either of them.

The Companies Law also regulates the liability of directors and members of the board of directors. Article 201 states that:

> The chairman and the members of the board of directors are responsible towards the company, its shareholders and any third party for any acts of fraud or misuse of power, for any violations of the law and the Company Contract and any management errors.

This is particularly important as most securities law violations are a result of actions by the members of the board of directors.[31] The legislature has attempted to regulate their behaviour wherever possible.

The Companies Law furthermore seeks to protect the shareholders and to enable them to file a liability lawsuit. Article 204 states:

> Any shareholder shall be entitled to personally file a liability claim on behalf of the company, in case the company fails to file such a claim. In this case, the company shall be made party to the claim in order to obtain a judgment of compensation in its favour. Furthermore, a shareholder may file his personal claim of compensation, if the error has caused him damages. Any stipulation in the Company Contract to the contrary shall be null and void.

## 3.4 Accounting Laws

Companies are required to report their earnings in published financial statements. Due to the number of accounting scandals during the late 1990s and the early 2000s, which caused huge losses to shareholders of securities,[32] various laws and regulations had to be enacted. These scandals have often been referred to as 'cooking the books' or 'accounting games'.[33]

---

31 Article 304 of the Companies Law regulates the responsibility of the directors and managers by introducing penalties for violations of the law, 'Without prejudice to a more severe penalty provided for in any other law, any of the following shall be punished with imprisonment for a term not exceeding one year and a fine of not less than five thousand Dinars and not exceeding ten thousand Dinars or either of these two penalties…4. Any member of the board of directors, manager or liquidator who in such capacity exploited with mala fide intent the company's assets or shares to gain directly or indirectly a personal benefit for himself or for a third party'.

32 Henry R Cheeseman (n 78) 633.

33 Roger L Martin, *Fixing The Game: How Runaway Expectations Broke the Economy and How to Get Back to Reality* (Harvard Business Review Press 2011) 86.

Those who are involved in securities activities rely on financial statements to make informed decisions on how best to invest money. Financial statements include an income statement, balance sheet, statement of shareholders' equity, statement of cash flows, management's discussion and analysis of financial condition, and results of operation. Since investors rely on these documents, it is imperative that they be accurate and trustworthy. Any misrepresentation or falsehood can have far-reaching consequences.

Investors in securities tend to look at published annual reports and accounts, such as balance sheets,[34] profit and loss accounts,[35] and cash flow statements[36] for reassurance. It is presumed that annual reports and audited financial records represent a company's true financial standing or health. However, as recent corporate failures have demonstrated, financial statements, even audited ones, have proved to be unreliable. Below is a list of techniques that have been used to 'cook the books'[37] to mislead investors in securities.

(i) *Off-balance-sheet vehicles.*
   Liabilities and assets are not included on a balance sheet. One way of doing this is to buy another company and then have the other company borrow money.
(ii) *Capitalising expenses.*
   This involves treating an expense as if it were capital. For example, Worldcom crashed because the company capitalised expenses to show a large profit that did not exist. The company put the expenses on the balance sheet as assets; they should have been in the profit and loss statement. The company treated the expenses as assets to show falsely that it had substantial assets; in fact, these were not assets but operational costs.

---

34 A balance sheet is defined as a financial statement, which shows an assets account (fixed and current assets) and liability account as of a fixed date, and the balance sheet must balance. Roger Mason, *Bookkeeping and Accounting in a Week* (4th edn, Hodder Education 2012) 86.

35 A profit and loss account (P&L) is defined as a financial statement, which shows all of the revenue and expense items during a certain period, such as three, six, or 12 months; ibid 72.

36 The cash flow statement concerns the money coming into and out of the business relating to operations, investing, and financing. It is important because it shows the profits on paper and the cash in the bank. Richard Baker, *Short Introduction to Accounting* (CUP 2011) 31–39.

37 Lee Ann Obringer, 'How Cooking the Books Works' <http://money.howstuffworks.com/cooking-books1.htm>.

(iii) *Manipulating the timing of expenses.*

Income can be taken only when there are invoices. Consequently, if a contract is over a period of time, the revenue and cost also must be over a period of time. However, some companies try to put all the revenue and expenses into the profit and loss account when they sign a contract.

Other examples:

- Recording sales just after the order but before the goods are shipped.
- Recording income without considering goods returns strategy.
- Not recording discounts.

(iv) *Non-recurring expenses and pension manipulation.*

A company guarantees to pay an employee a specific amount based on a final salary and years of service. To guarantee this, companies must put money in a fund and invest it. One safe investment is a cash bond, which pays interest and secures the capital. However, some companies invest in the stock exchange, which involves more risk. They forecast by how much the interest will appreciate and calculate their contributions accordingly. They might underestimate their contribution to keep their profit high. If the fund does not grow sufficiently, there will not be enough money to pay pensions; this is known as a 'hole' in the pension fund. An example of this is the Royal Mail case.[38]

Some of the above problems are compounded by poor auditing, as in the case of Enron. The auditor Arthur Andersen knew about the accounting fraud but did nothing about it. They were found guilty of destroying documents related to Enron's auditing.[39] To stop this kind of fraud, accounting laws require firms to follow accounting reporting standards when they prepare their financial reports. It is also important to have auditing standards and to have a public body to oversee the auditing profession. Accurate and reliable published accounts reduce the risks of an investor making a poor investment decision.[40] However, it is not easy as it is complex and there is a financial cost to complying.

In the UK, since 1947 companies have had to follow the UK accounting framework Generally Accepted Accounting Principles (GAAP) to present

---

38  'Royal Mail IPO: A Windfall to Fill a Hole?' <http://blogs.wsj.com/moneybeat/2013/09/12/royal-mail-ipo-a-windfall-to-fill-a-hole/>.

39  544 US 696 (2005).

40  <https://frc.org.uk/Our-Work/Publications/Accounting-and-Reporting-Policy/FRS-102-The-Financial-Reporting-Standard-appli-(1).pdf >.

a 'true and fair view' (TFV).[41] In 2005, GAAP required public companies to follow International Financial Reporting Standards (IFRSs).[42] The Audit Directive has two important points. First, an auditor must express their opinion on the statement of compliance with legal requirements. Second, an auditor must state whether any material mistake has been identified. The Financial Reporting Council (FRC), as a single independent entity, sets and enforces the accounting framework and judges the fair and true view of the financial statements that show the firm's position, profit, and loss.

In the US, accounting laws and rules are passed by various federal, state, and self-regulatory organisations (SROs). The accounting rules created for listed companies are subject to the Securities and Exchange Commission's oversight. The SEC has relied on SROs to create financial reporting standards for listed companies. These are known as Generally Accepted Accounting Principles (GAAP) that were established by the Financial Accounting Standards Board (FASB).

The Sarbanes-Oxley Act 2002 (SOX) created the Public Company Accounting Oversight Board (PCAOB) to oversee the auditing function for listed companies. The SEC has oversight over the FASB and the PCAOB.

Listed companies are required to file annual reports with the following people and institutions:

1) *The SEC*: companies need to provide an annual report to the SEC setting out all regulated transactions and providing them with accounting records as needed. Listed companies must provide an annual report to the SEC called Form-10-K. Before 2007, both foreign and domestic listed companies were required to file the report with the SEC.

2) *Shareholders*: companies need to account to the shareholders for all amounts handled in the normal course of business. The SEC requires the annual report created by listed companies to be sent to shareholders including more details such as a letter from the CEO, financial data, results of operations, market segment information, new product plans, subsidiary activities, and research and development on future programs. The SEC also requires listed companies to post their annual reports on the listed company website. Companies may send their annual 10-K report to shareholders instead of creating a separate annual report.

---

41  Companies Act 1947, s13 and s16; Companies Act 2006, s396(2) states that 'the accounts must give a true and fair view'.

42  <http://www.icaew.com/en/library/subject-gateways/accounting-standards/knowledge-guide-to-international-accounting-standards>.

3) *The report of the external auditor*: the main purpose of an external audit process is to ensure that the information provided by the company is accurate and free from material misstatements that are caused by error or fraud. The external auditor must give his opinion on the financial statements as well as make any other comments and recommendations as may be required.

4) *Internal control report*: companies need to prepare this document setting out details of the internal audit system and the risk management process. According to the SOX Act, listed companies are required to include details in their annual reports pertaining to the internal controls systems of the company. Section 404 of SOX requires management at public companies to select an internal control framework and then assess and report annually on the design and operating effectiveness of their internal controls.

In Kuwait, there is no specific legal code providing for accounting laws. However, there are references to accounting matters in other pieces of legislation. The Companies Law makes specific references to auditors, especially external auditors, whereas the securities law makes reference to the internal auditor. These auditors are required to conduct themselves according to international standards, even though these are not codified into Kuwaiti law. The role of the auditor in Kuwait is set out in Law No 1 of 2016 dealing with company law. Articles 227 to 233 set out the regulations pertaining to the audit profession and its role in Kuwait.

An external auditor is engaged by the business to audit the financial reporting to confirm its reliability. The Companies Law 2016 Article 227 requires that:

> The Public Shareholding Company shall have one or more auditors to be appointed by the ordinary general meeting following approval of Central Bank of Kuwait with regard to companies subject to its supervision.

Once appointed, the external auditor maintains professional independence and performs their work without interference. After completion of the audit, the auditor submits a report on the company's financial statements and confirms whether such statements reflect the company's balance sheet at the end of the financial year and the results of the company for such year. Furthermore, they will state whether the data contained in the board of directors' report is consistent with the facts established in the company's accounting records and documents.

According to Article 230 of the Companies Law the auditor's report must include specific items such as:

1. That the company maintains accurate and proper accounting records.
2. That the auditor has been given proper access to these records in order to carry out their work.
3. That the accounting records reflect the true state of affairs of the company.
4. That the company has complied with all legal requirements imposed by law.
5. That the accounting records are maintained in line with the best practice standards.
6. Whether there have been violations of the provisions of the law or the company contract during the financial year and whether these violations still exist, to the extent such information is made available to the auditor.
7. All other relevant information pertaining to the financial management of the company that the auditor deems necessary.

The work of the auditor is so important that the Act, Article 232, confers liability for any damage sustained by the company, the shareholders, or others due to a fault committed in the course and by reason of their work to the auditor.

The role of the internal auditor has not been clarified until recently. Without proper regulation and legislation, there was widespread controversy about this subject. Recently, the role of internal auditing has become more important. The internal auditing function is part of corporate governance principles. An internal audit system is an independent and objective assurance and advisory activity that aims to increase value and enhance the organisation's functions.

In Kuwait, the scope of the internal audit process includes:

1. Auditing to ensure the soundness of the financial statements.
2. The efficiency of the company's activities.
3. Evaluation of the extent and commitment to supervisory measures.

According to the 2010 Act, the Kuwaiti authority has the power to determine the kind of accounting standards which companies must follow.[43] According

---

43 Capital Market Law 2010, Article 68.

to Rule No 10/2011 the authority has adopted the International Financial Reporting Standards (IFRSs) issued by the International Accounting Standards Board (IASB). However, several experts in the accounting field have criticised the application of international accounting standards, saying that it is difficult to comply with these rules because of complexities. They recommended creating an independent body to help apply and supervise this complicated process.[44]

Protecting investors in securities requires good accounting legislation that is fairly presented and subject to professional judgment. There are three important points to cover. First, having good accounting reporting standards. The second point is having professional auditors that express their opinion and state any misstatement. The third requirement is having a single independent body to set and enforce accounting standards.

Although in Kuwait there is a clear indication of what is expected of companies in terms of financial reporting, it is difficult to measure their compliance because of the lack of a specific body to measure them. Kuwait needs to have a body responsible for developing the accounting standards and making firms comply, such as the Financial Reporting Council (FRC) in the UK.

---

44  <www.alanba.com.kw/ar/economy-news/363546/26-02-2013>.

# 4 Stock Exchanges

A stock exchange is defined as 'a marketplace in which shares, securities, commodities, derivatives and other financial instruments are traded'.[1] Trading on stock exchanges is a way for companies to raise money by selling shares of ownership in the company. Trading in securities is beneficial for buyers as they are easily bought and sold and allow for large increases in the value of invested capital and the protection of capital from the negative effects of taxation and inflation.

Stock exchanges or stock markets differ significantly from other commercial markets and, as a result, their effective performance demands the implementation of a regulatory framework in the form of securities regulations. These are unlike the laws that govern other ordinary, non-securities-related commercial dealings.

This chapter considers the stock exchanges in the UK, the US, and Kuwait. It focuses on how each exchange started and how it has grown to what it is today. Furthermore, consideration is given to how each country chooses to regulate its stock exchanges and sales of securities. Lastly, it deals with the proposals by academics and critics for the best way to regulate a stock exchange.

## 4.1 Historical Development of Stock Exchanges

The history of stock markets can be traced back to 1602 when the world's first formal stock exchange was created in Amsterdam. The Dutch East India company began offering stocks and bonds on the Amsterdam bourse in 1602 and became the first company listed on the stock exchange when it was launched in 1611. After the success of the Amsterdam Stock Market, the idea of creating other stock markets spread rapidly around the world.

---

1 Thomas Anthony Guerriero (n 10) 58.

DOI: 10.4324/9781003301875-5

### 4.1.1  UK Stock Exchanges

The London Stock Exchange is one of the oldest stock markets in the world and can trace its origins back several centuries. During the seventeenth century, a broker named Jonathan Castaing began operating from Jonathan's Coffee House. There, he published listing prices of commodities that included such things as salt, coal, and paper. By 1698 he was publishing a list of currency, stock, and commodity prices that included gold, ducats, silver staters, and pieces of eight. Trade in these commodities and other merchandise by public auction was the start of organised trading in London.

During the Industrial Revolution, the world economy grew rapidly and lending to foreign countries became a profitable business. The sale of foreign securities was one of the first major areas of development for trading on the stock exchange. Due to the economic benefits of trading in securities and stocks, other exchanges in cities such as Manchester and Liverpool opened in due course.

As a result of widespread fraud during this period, a rule book had to be published to set out the rules and regulations pertaining to the sale of commodities and securities. This 'First Rule Book' was published in 1812, setting out rules relating to settlement and default as well as other related matters.

During the 1800s and early 1900s, the UK became embroiled in many wars against the French, Dutch, and other nations. Imperialism also required the British government to raise capital to fund its military operations around the world. Particularly during the First World War, the stock exchange played a crucial role in the liquidation of almost a quarter of the British overseas securities to finance the war effort.

Over the course of the twentieth century, the UK Stock Exchange has grown from strength to strength. Some of the most notable developments occurred in 1973 when the regional exchanges were merged to form the Stock Exchange of Great Britain and Ireland, later renamed the London Stock Exchange (LSE). In 1986, the market was de-regulated and computerised trading replaced the previous trading floor method. This period became known as the 'Big Bang' due to the huge increase in trading on the exchange.

In 1995, the Alternative Investment Market (AIM) was launched to give smaller companies access to investors. Initially, only ten companies were traded on this market, but it has since grown substantially. The AIM allowed smaller growing companies access to international markets and by 2017 over 1,000 companies were trading on this market.

Other notable developments include the merging of the London Stock Exchange with the Italian Stock Exchange in 2007. Furthermore, in 2019 the Shanghai–London Stock Connect partnership was launched. This led to the development of a cross-listing mechanism between the two exchanges which enables London-listed corporates to issue Chinese Depositary Receipts in Shanghai and Shanghai-listed corporates to issue Global Depository Receipts in London.

### 4.1.2 Stock Exchanges in the US

The stock exchange in the US had its beginnings in the Revolutionary War when the US government needed to raise funds for the war effort. To raise the required capital, the government issued bonds or promissory notes, with a promise to repay the money in the future. After the war ended in 1783, the holders of these promissory notes began to exchange them for immediate payment. Merchants saw this as an opportunity and recognised a need for a formal exchange to trade in these and other commodities.

In 1792, 24 stockbrokers from New York created the New York Stock Exchange. The agreement to create the exchange was signed under a buttonwood tree on Wall Street in New York City and became known as the Buttonwood Agreement. The purpose of this agreement was to bring order to the notoriously disorganised and chaotic trading market.

Whilst stock exchanges opened in cities such as Chicago, Los Angeles, and Philadelphia, it was the New York Stock Exchange that became the most powerful. The location of the exchange led to its speedy growth. It was in the heart of all the business and trade coming to and going from the United States, as well as the domestic base for most banks and large corporations. By setting listing requirements and demanding fees, the New York Stock Exchange became a very wealthy institution.

In addition to the NYSE, the American Stock Exchange became another important exchange. The AMEX was initially known as the 'Curb Exchange' where so-called Curbstone brokers would invest in smaller, newer companies. This trade allowed many companies to grow and promoted the American entrepreneurial spirit. The AMEX eventually joined the NYSE group of exchanges in 2008.

The NYSE was less encumbered by regulation than the Stock Exchange in the UK. This, together with the rapid growth in the American economy, led to the exchange becoming the most important stock exchange in the world. During the early stages of the twentieth century, the US economy enjoyed an extended period of prosperity that led many companies to list on the NYSE. However, with the Wall Street Crash and Great Depression of the 1930s the stock market lost 85% of its total value. Many companies were forced to declare bankruptcy or shut down.

Today, the New York Stock Exchange is the largest exchange in the world, in terms of capitalised trading volume, and is five times the size of

NASDAQ. However, the exchange is the fourth largest in number of listings behind the Bombay, London, and NASDAQ exchanges. Even though many other countries have their own stock exchanges, companies that wish to trade internationally will still list on the NYSE.

### 4.1.2.1 Indices

The S&P 500, the NASDAQ, and the Dow Jones Industrial Average (Dow Jones) are market indices that reflect how the market is performing. Of these, the Dow Jones is the oldest. It is comprised solely of 30 large-cap companies that represent a huge array of American businesses. The companies within this index are huge, so large in fact that it can be said that they represent the state of the US economy.

The S&P 500 represents the movements of the broader markets. The index covers the largest companies that trade on the NYSE, chosen on a few basic criteria. Companies within this index are required to trade at sufficient volume with adequate market liquidity, have a market cap of over US$ 5 billion and have at least 50% of the company's stock available on the public float.

The NASDAQ is a separate stock exchange that is traded electronically. Typically, the companies listed on the NASDAQ Composite Index are tech companies, but it does also include a small number of other non-tech companies.

### 4.1.3  Kuwaiti Stock Exchange

Prior to the Second World War, no transactions involving securities occurred in Kuwait. The discovery of a vast supply of oil significantly transformed the lives of the Kuwaiti people, who previously lived simply. Before the discovery of oil, the Kuwaiti economy relied on the pearl trade, maritime transport, and fishing.[2] A tribe of Bedouins lived in the desert and herded sheep and camels. Since 1946, oil has dominated the Kuwaiti economy and has ultimately displaced traditional activities.[3] Land trade and real estate were the main forms of wealth during the transitional period.[4]

---

2  Hazem El-Beblawi and Raed Fahmy, *Kuwait's Stock Market* (Chamber of Kuwait Commerce and Industry 1982) [6] 22.

3  Ibid.

4  Ayman Abdul-hadi, *Stock Markets of the Arabic world: Trends, Problems and Prospects for Integration* (Routledge 1988) 20.

After this period of transition to an oil economy, the first Kuwait public company was established in 1952, which was called the National Bank. The National Cinema Company and the Kuwait Oil Tankers Company were established in 1954 and 1957, respectively.[5] In 1960, the Commercial Companies Act No 15 was passed to encourage people to invest in corporations including 13 public companies established by the government. This law was the first to organise the issuance of shares by companies and subscribers to these shares.[6] This was followed by Law No 32 in 1970 which was enacted to regulate the negotiation and transaction of company securities. At that time, there were few companies and there was a lack of sufficient knowledge about dealing in securities.

The Kuwait Stock Exchange officially began in October 1983 with the passage of a law aimed at coordinating the trading of stocks through several Kuwaiti shareholding companies that eventually became the precursor of the KSE. The formation of the Kuwait Clearing Company in 1982 directly led to the formal establishment of the modern-day Kuwait Stock Exchange in 1983, although the KSE still remains an arm of the Kuwaiti government. Since then, the exchange has grown steadily to become a leading player among the Middle East securities-trading markets and by 2006 it had become one of the Middle East's leading exchanges.

The 2007–2008 global financial crisis affected the Kuwait stock market extremely negatively. Companies whose shares were listed on the KSE saw their overall net profits plummet and by 2009, 24 of the 204 listed companies on KSE were delisted for not posting year-end results.

Law No 32 gave the Minister of Commerce and Trade the power to issue the necessary rules to regulate the trading of securities of Kuwaiti firms. These rules were based on the opinion of the Market Committee (MC).[7] The first market committee was established in 1976.[8] In 1977 a stock exchange was initiated in Kuwait, which was the important first step along the path of trading securities in Kuwait.[9] The stock exchange was intended to replace unofficial unregulated stock exchanges.

---

5 Yacoub Sarkhouh, *Shares Trading in the Stock Market in Joint Stock Companies in Accordance with Kuwaiti Law* (2nd edn, Foundation Library 1993–1994) 8.
6 Amid Salam, *Managing Crisis in the Arab and Global Stock Exchanges and Sustainable Development* (Abu Dhabi 2002) 181.
7 The Market Committee consists of eight members. The chairman is the Minister of Commerce and Trade. It has representatives of the Ministry of Finance and the Central Bank of Kuwait. It also has five Kuwaiti citizens with expertise and competence in financial matters.
8 Khaled Helmy (n 33) 155.
9 Ibid 182.

Kuwait was the first country in the region to establish a legal framework for its Stock Exchange. After the Suq al-Manakh[10] Crisis in 1983, the Kuwaiti legislature issued the Emiri Decree Organising Kuwait Stock Exchange No 35, which sought to protect public savings and investors' interests. In 1983, the Kuwait Stock Exchange became an independent body recognised by Emiri Decree No 20/1983. During that same year, Emiri Decree No 35/1983 was passed. This included stock exchange objectives, the listing and acceptance of securities, stock exchange membership, dealing in securities, stock exchange administration, stock exchange budget and financial accounts, disputes and arbitration, and disciplinary action. The most important change came with Article No 1, which provided that the Stock Exchange should be an independent entity.

In April 2014, the Boursa Kuwait was established by the Capital Markets Authority Commissioners' Council Resolution No 37/2013. Two years later, in 2016, it was entrusted with the operation of the Kuwait Stock Exchange and to practise the activity of a securities exchange. In taking control of the securities exchange, it replaced the former Kuwait stock exchange.

In 2019, the first phase of privatisation of the Boursa commenced, when a consortium comprised of international exchanges and a group of Kuwaiti investment companies were awarded the bid for a 44% equity stake in Boursa Kuwait. In December 2019, the privatisation process was finalised after the initial public offering of the Capital Markets Authority's 50% stake in the company was offered to Kuwaiti citizens.[11]

The Boursa Kuwait is comprised of two main markets. The 'Premier Market' targets companies with high liquidity and a medium to large market capitalisation. Companies listed on this market are available in the 'Premier' and 'All-Share' market indices. The other market is known as the 'Main Market', which is comprised of companies that do not qualify to be listed in the Premier Market. Some companies that do not comply with all the listing rules or qualify according to the conditions of the Premier Market are listed under the Main Market. Once compliance has been completed, they can be listed on the Premier Market.

The Boursa Kuwait Main Market 50 Index is a Market Capitalisation Weighted Index that reflects the top 50 companies in the Main Market. The index's inclusions and exclusions are based on the calculation of the average daily traded value (ADTV). The index constituents are reviewed on an annual basis.[12]

---

10  Selling and buying animals, such as goats and sheep, was the main function of this market.
11  <www.boursakuwait.com.kw/en/history>.
12  <www.boursakuwait.com.kw/en/securities/indices/bk-main-50.>.

This distinction between the two markets and their indices pertains to the different qualifying criteria imposed on companies. These listings are reviewed annually and are influenced by corporate actions such as mergers and acquisitions. However, all listed companies are subject to securities laws and related laws as enforced by the Capital Markets Authority.

## 4.2 Stock Exchanges and Securities Laws

Trading in securities on the various stock exchanges has many advantages and disadvantages. Due to unscrupulous practices by traders and investors, governments around the world have enacted legislation to regulate stock exchanges. This section of the book focuses on whether regulation of stock markets is necessary, how it is done in reality, and ways in which it can be improved.

### 4.2.1 Is Regulation of a Stock Exchange Necessary?

Whether regulation is necessary or not depends on one's point of view. There are arguments for and against the regulation of the markets. One of the arguments against market regulation is the so-called 'efficient markets theory'. According to this theory, 'the stock prices always reflect all available information and are efficient prices'.[13] This means that no one can achieve extraordinary profits at the expense of another party. Prices are always equal to the true value of the assets. The prices are the outcomes of the views of all investors. The efficient markets theory is based on the laws that describe the behaviour of markets where the price is set by supply and demand and by external shocks, which, in financial markets, means new information.[14] This theory does not consider price movements that might result from market abuse.

One critic of this theory is Robert Shiller, who said that the efficient markets theory is only half true. He questioned the assertions that securities' prices reflect the true value of assets.[15] Another critic, George Cooper, also criticised the efficient markets theory as being 'more faith than fact' and asserted that it does not work for all markets.[16] In financial markets, a power pushes the markets away from equilibrium that causes 'financial markets

---

13  Ibid 156.
14  George Cooper, *The Origin of Financial Crises: Central Banks, Credit Bubbles and The Efficient Fallacy* (Harriman House 2010) 9.
15  Robert Shiller (37).
16  George Cooper (n 114) 4.

to behave in a way that is inconsistent with the theory of efficient markets'.[17] In financial markets, the forces pushing the price are not explained by the efficient markets theory. For example, a lack of supply leads to an increase in demand, and asset prices move because of increased demand.[18] He blamed the academic community for promoting the efficient markets theory to self-regulate markets.[19] The reality is that regulation is necessary.

An argument put forward for why regulation is necessary is Hyman P Minsky's theory known as the 'financial instability hypothesis'. The most important difference between this theory and the efficient markets theory is the forces that are believed to cause prices to move. The efficient markets theory mentions that any change of price is a result of external shocks, which, in financial markets, is new information. However, the financial instability hypothesis states that, in addition to external forces, there are internal forces that do not lead financial markets to stability, to self-optimisation, or towards a natural optimal allocation of resources.[20]

Economists spend their lives formulating theories about markets and their regulation. This book does not purport to be an academic discussion about such theories. The need for regulation is obvious, as evidenced by numerous financial crises and scandals, from which Kuwait is not immune. Regardless of the theories, the reality is that financial crises have occurred, people have suffered as a result, and this could have been avoided by having sound regulations in place. There is a greater development towards intervention in and regulation of the markets.[21]

In the financial literature, the risks facing investors can be divided into two main types. The first is direct risks which arise from market abuse, irresponsible actions by individuals or companies, and poor corporate governance by companies. The second is indirect risks which are due to the instability of the financial system. For instance, if a bank goes bankrupt then it affects investors indirectly.

Three main types of direct risks are cited in the financial literature.

(i)  First, the risk that someone will abuse the market. Examples of this are insider dealing or manipulation of the share prices or supplying false information.

---

17  Ibid 158.
18  Ibid 14.
19  Ibid 175.
20  Ibid 13.
21  Mathieu Deflem, *Sociology of Law Vision of a Scholarly Tradition* (CUP 2010) 152.

(ii) Second, risk due to irresponsible actions, usually by companies who do not disclose information on time or make incomplete disclosure.
(iii) Third, risk from poor corporate governance where managers or directors misbehave.

Protection against these risks is provided by different types of regulation. Protection against market abuse is by means of so-called 'hard law'. This consists of primary legislation, such as acts of parliament, and secondary legislation, which is legislation delegated by an act of parliament.

Secondary legislation consists of so-called 'rules'. It is especially useful because it is enacted quickly and saves parliamentary time. It is passed by people who understand the subject and it has the power to impose fines without the need to go to court. Irresponsible actions are also dealt with by hard law in the form of secondary legislation. Corporate governance, on the other hand, is protected by so-called 'soft law'. It is considered to be 'soft' because an offender cannot be jailed or fined. This soft law consists of voluntary codes that are agreed to by organisations and companies. Soft law will be discussed further in Chapter 9 of this book.

There are many other examples that show the need to regulate the stock exchange. Recently, financial markets (including stock exchanges) have become more complex because of technological development, innovative financial instruments, and globalisation. This increases the need to regulate the stock exchange to protect individual investors. Without regulating the market, individual investors would suffer.

## 4.3 How Is the Stock Market Regulated Today?

Stock exchange regulation is a process that aims to deal with the complex set of business risks faced by companies and consumers alike. This section focuses on how stock markets are regulated in different countries.

### 4.3.1 Stock Exchanges in the UK

The Financial Conduct Authority (FCA) is the agency responsible for the regulation of securities in the UK. The UK Financial Services and Markets Act 2000 (FSMA) is the principal piece of legislation regulating the trade in securities in the UK. In addition, the FCA sets out in its handbook the rules and guidance (the FCA Handbook) relating to:

• The Listing Rules (LRs).

- The Prospectus Rules (PRs), which implement the EU Prospectus Directive in the UK and set out the content requirements for prospectuses.
- The Disclosure and Transparency Rules (DTRs), which implement sections of the EU Transparency Directive and make other rules concerning the transparency of and access to information in the UK financial markets including aspects of the EU Market Abuse Regulation (MAR).

The FCA has as its stated aim:

1) Ensuring stability and resilience, access, effectiveness, and predictability; fairness and cleanliness; and the prevention of financial crimes.
2) Securing appropriate degrees of protection for those who use or participate in markets.
3) Promoting effective competition between providers of goods and services in the interests of market users.

### 4.3.1.1 EU Regulations

In addition to UK legislation, several EU regulations that govern securities offerings apply directly in the UK. These include the following:

(i) *Market Abuse Regulation (MAR)*: these regulations apply to behaviour or transactions in securities that are admitted to trading on a Multilateral Trading Facility (MTF) or regulated market (or for which a request for admission to trading has been made) or traded on an MTF or Organised Trading Facility (OTF), and securities whose price or value depends on or influences the price or value of such securities. The MAR establishes an EU-wide regulatory framework on insider dealing, the unlawful disclosure of inside information and market manipulation (market abuse), as well as measures to prevent market abuse to ensure the integrity of financial markets in the EU and to enhance investor protection and confidence in those markets.

(ii) *EU Packaged Retail and Insurance-Based Investment Products Regulation (PRIIPs)*: this regulation prohibit securities within its scope from being offered or otherwise made available to retail investors in any EU member state unless a key information document has been prepared and published in accordance with PRIIPs. Securities are within the scope of PRIIPs if they constitute an investment where, regardless of its legal form, the amount repayable to the retail investor is subject to fluctuations because of exposure to reference values or to the performance of one or more assets that are not directly purchased by the retail investor, or an insurance-based investment product that offers a maturity or surrender value that is wholly or partially exposed, directly or indirectly, to market fluctuations.

### 4.3.2 US Stock Exchanges

It is important to understand the meaning and definition of the term exchange as it is used in laws and regulations. The 1934 Securities Act codified the common term and in Section 3 (a)(1) defines the exchange as:

> The term 'exchange' means any organization, association, or group of persons, whether incorporated or unincorporated, which constitutes, maintains, or provides a market place or facilities for bringing together purchasers and sellers of Securities or for otherwise performing with respect to securities, the functions commonly performed by a stock exchange as that term is generally understood, and includes the market place and the market facilities maintained by such exchange.

The New York Stock Exchange is the main stock exchange in the US. It is a self-regulating organisation, but it is still subject to government oversight in the form of the Securities and Exchange Commission (SEC). The SEC is the government body that oversees the rules and rule changes of the NYSE.

The NYSE Regulation Market Surveillance Division (NYSER) is responsible for monitoring activities on the NYSE's equities, options, and bonds markets and for addressing non-compliance with the exchange's rules and federal securities laws. The NYSER enforces both the exchange rules and any federal securities requirements. It also monitors and enforces listed companies' compliance with applicable listing standards of the exchange. Furthermore, it is also responsible for market surveillance to detect any unlawful and unethical behaviour of stockbrokers and listed companies.

The SEC was created to enable the US government to oversee the trade in securities and equities in the stock exchange, with a view to protecting investors. The goal of the SEC is to create financial transparency for public companies and to hold them accountable for all business and financial transactions. All public companies, including those that trade securities on the NYSE must file annual and quarterly financial reports with the SEC.

Generally, issues of securities offered in interstate commerce must be registered with the SEC before they can be sold to investors. Financial services firms (FSF) must also register with the SEC to conduct business. These include broker-dealers, advisory firms, and asset managers, as well as their professional representatives. The primary function of the SEC is to oversee organisations and individuals in the securities markets. They can establish securities rules and regulations.

The SEC promotes disclosure and sharing of market-related information, fair dealing, and protection against fraud. It provides investors with access to registration statements, periodic financial reports, and other securities forms through its electronic data-gathering, analysis, and retrieval database, known as EDGAR. This is the electronic filing system created by the SEC to increase the efficiency and accessibility of corporate filings.

### 4.3.3 The Kuwait Stock Exchange

In 2010, a new era relating to stock exchanges was introduced by passing the Capital Market Law 2010. This created two different bodies: the Capital Market Authority and the Stock Exchange Body.

The functions of the Authority are not limited to its role of supervising the Kuwait Stock Exchange but transcend it to exercise supervision and control of all the elements of the capital markets, from licensing incorporation to practice and to liquidation of all the companies operating in these markets. The system of dealing with securities must follow the procedures and rules set by the Exchange and approved by the Authority.

According to the Act, the role of the Exchange is that:

> An Exchange runs a trading system designated to match Bid and Ask Offers for securities that are listed on the Exchange.[22]

The Exchange is managed by a Board of Directors formed of a Chairman and a Vice Chairman, and six members.[23]

According to Article 1.4.1 of the Executive Bylaws 2015 of the 2010 Act:

> The Exchange shall abide by the following obligations:
>
> 1) Set policies and procedures to ensure the fairness, transparency, and efficiency in trading in listed securities.
> 2) Ensure that management maintains proper awareness of the risks associated with its business and operations.
> 3) Set policies and procedures to determine and manage any conflicts of interest between the Exchange and its members or among shareholders or management.

---

22  Article 1.2.1 of the Executive Bylaws 2015.
23  Article 1.3.1 of the Executive Bylaws 2015.

4) Provide and operate its services in accordance with applicable laws and regulations.
5) Organize its operations, standards of practice and its members' behaviour in accordance with the rules, policies and procedures of the Exchange.
6) Set preventive measures to ensure the sound management of the technical operation of its systems, including the establishment of effective contingency arrangements to cope with the risks of system disruptions.
7) Provide its services in accordance with the most advanced techniques and applications and automated systems in line with the international standards approved and set by the Authority.
8) Maintain sufficient financial resources to facilitate the performance of its business in a regulated form.
9) Maintain the confidentiality of all information under its custody with respect to its members, issuers and clients. It is not permissible to disclose such information except to the Authority, or by its order or by a judicial order. It shall set policies and procedures to protect the information systems.
10) Follow the Authority's instructions.

The Kuwaiti Stock Exchange can enforce penalties against any listed companies. Article 42 of the 2010 Act mentions that:

The Exchange shall form a committee to be entrusted with regard to the violations committed by any of its Members. The Authority shall issue the regulations and controls necessary for its work and for Members. The committee may impose the following penalties:

1) Cautioning the violator to discontinue committing the violation.
2) Issuing a warning.
3) Subjecting the violator to further supervision.
4) Suspension from working or practicing the profession for a period not exceeding one year.
5) Imposing restrictions on the violator's activity or activities.
6) Suspension of trading of a security for a specific period in the interest of the market. In all cases, the committee may cancel transactions related to the violation and the consequences thereof.

In 2015, the amendment of Article 33 of Law 2010 was based on its relevance to the establishment of the Securities Exchange Company in view of its being a shareholding company. The authority has the power to approve licensing for other securities exchanges whose capital, activity, and business and management restrictions and conditions are determined through a resolution by the Board of Commissioners.

## 4.4 How Should the Stock Exchange Be Regulated?

There are several models for regulating stock exchanges.

The first model of regulation is self-regulation. The nature, scope, and structure of self-regulation have changed greatly over the last 20 years and there is no clear definition of it. There is a range of self-regulatory forms the world over. Sometimes, the term self-regulation is used to refer to formal self-regulatory organisations (SROs). An SRO can be described as 'a private institution that establishes, monitors compliance with, and enforces rules applicable to Securities markets and the conduct of the SRO's members'.[24] An SRO is 'a non-governmental organisation that has the power to create and enforce industry regulations and standards'.[25] It is part-way between zero regulation and state regulation, under which the state specifies, administers, and enforces the regulations. Any person who wants to be a member of the SRO must be prepared to follow its rules.[26]

Self-regulatory organisations, such as stock exchanges, govern themselves without outside interference, especially if they are responsible for the operation of the exchange. This includes: 1) regulating market transactions, including ensuring that the members' actions are in accordance with pre-agreed rules; 2) regulating the market participants by ensuring that they do not breach their obligations and that they maintain the value of their capital over time, that they do not take excessive risk, that they do not breach ethical behaviour, and that if they breach their obligations, they face sanctions from the SRO itself; and 3) that dispute resolution and enforcement actions are provided, including private mechanisms that enforce good conduct.[27] In some cases, the internal statutory rules involve determining the financial sources, managers' and employees' codes of conduct, oversight procedures, and the formal structure of the SROs.[28]

---

24  John Carson, 'Self-Regulation in Securities Markets' (Working Paper for World Bank Financial Sector Policy Group 2010) 1.
25  Thomas Anthony Guerriero (n 10) 58.
26  Ruben Lee, *What Is An Exchange? The Automation, Management, and Regulation of Financial Markets* (OUP 2000) 129.
27  Biagio Bossone and Larry Promisel, 'The Role of Financial Self-Regulation in Developing Economies' (The World Bank) <www1.worldbank.org/finance/html/self-regulation-in-developing-.html>.
28  Ibid.

Self-regulation has several advantages: 1) greater ability to monitor effectively; 2) members of an SRO may have more interest in keeping the market safe and in preserving its integrity; 3) members of an SRO have more knowledge, expertise, and experience about the market; and 4) the SRO has more flexibility.[29]

The second model of regulation is public or governmental regulation. In recent times, many countries have transferred, in different degrees, some of the power and responsibility for regulation from the exchanges to a public regulator, which means that there is reduced reliance on exchanges as SROs.[30] Consequently, there are now four models of self-regulation involving the exchange and the regulator.

- The first is the 'government model', in which securities' regulation lies with a public authority, and the exchanges have limited supervision of their markets. This has occurred because of the movement of stock exchanges from non-profit-making to being profit-based and, in many instances, operating as a listed company.[31]
- The second is a 'limited exchange SRO', in which a primary regulator is a public authority, and the exchanges are responsible for operating functions, such as listing and supervising the markets.
- The third is the 'strong exchange model', in which a primary regulator is a public authority, and the exchanges have more operating functions, which include regulation of member conduct.
- The fourth is an 'independent member SRO', in which a primary regulator is a public authority that relies on an independent SRO for regulatory functions.[32]

Currently, many developed countries regulate their financial markets using the government model mentioned previously.[33] This is the case in Kuwait,

---

29  Ruben Lee (n 126) 190–191.
30  There are four important types of SROs in capital markets. The first are exchange SROs, such as securities exchanges with self-regulatory responsibility. The second are independent SROs, such as securities brokers or other intermediaries. The third are industry associations, such as bodies that provide best practices or guidance for members. The fourth is comprised of Central Securities depositories (CSDs) and clearing agencies. Exchange SROs are the most common in Securities markets. <www.world-exchanges.org/insight/views/self-regulation-Securities-markets>.
31  Iain G MacNeil (n 1) 24–25.
32  John Carson (n 124) 1–3.
33  'Self-Regulation in Today's Securities Markets: Outdated System or Work in Progress?' (2007) Working Paper, CFA Institute for Financial Market Integrity.

where the Kuwait Stock Exchange is a self-regulatory organisation, and the Capital Market Authority represents the government.

Therefore, it can be seen that because of the specialised nature of the topic, countries have found over time that in order to regulate dealing in the financial markets (including stock exchanges), it is better to appoint a 'financial authority' with rule-making and investigative power, and the power to enforce the securities laws through prosecution and/or the imposition of sanctions.

# 5  Regulatory Authority

As mentioned in the previous chapter, most securities that are traded are listed on the various stock exchanges around the world. To prevent abuse and criminals from taking advantage of investors and to regulate security activity, the various legislatures have enacted laws known as securities laws. Typically, these laws create a regulatory authority that is charged with overseeing or managing the trading in securities and the policing of any fraudulent behaviour. In terms of these laws, the regulatory authority has the power to enact rules and regulations that are applicable to their jurisdiction. These rules and the penalties associated with them are enforced by the regulatory authorities.

## 5.1  Regulatory Authority

This chapter will discuss the various bodies established in the countries of the UK, the US, and Kuwait, and their powers of rule-making and enforcement.

### 5.1.1  Regulatory Authority in the UK

The Financial Services Act 2012 created two regulators, the Financial Conduct Authority (FCA) and the Prudential Regulation Authority (PRA).[1] Although the FCA is not part of the Bank of England, the PRA is, and it is responsible for the supervision and the prudential regulation of banks, major investment firms, building societies, credit unions, and insurers, promoting safety and soundness to those firms and protecting policyholders.[2]

---

1  Financial Services Act 2012 sch 3A part 2.
2  <www.bankofengland.co.uk/pra/pages/default.aspx>.

DOI: 10.4324/9781003301875-6

The chair of the PRA is the Governor of the Bank of England, and the chief executive is the Deputy Governor for Prudential Regulation.[3]

The Financial Conduct Authority (FCA) regulates the financial markets, setting specific standards for the trade in securities. The FCA has as its primary aim 'making markets work well – for individuals, for business, large and small, and for the economy as a whole'. Having been established on 1 April 2013, the FCA took over responsibility for conduct and relevant prudential regulation from the Financial Services Authority. It is an independent public body funded entirely by the firms it regulates, by charging certain fees.

The Financial Conduct Authority (FCA) has been created as a separate institution from the Bank of England to regulate the conduct of financial services firms. The FCA's duties include preventing market abuse and ensuring that financial firms treat their customers fairly. Its three major objectives are:

1) Protecting consumers.
2) Promoting the integrity of the financial system.
3) Promoting effective competition.

It is also responsible for the micro-prudential regulation of those financial services that are not supervised by the PRA, such as, for example, asset managers, hedge funds, many brokers, dealers, independent financial advisers, and listed companies.

In addition to the FCA, the Prudential Regulation Authority (PRA) regulates banks, building societies, credit unions, insurers, and major investment firms. As a prudential regulator, it has a general objective to promote the safety and soundness of the firms it regulates.

In the UK, the board that governs the FCA is appointed by several parties.[4] A chair (non-executive member), a chief executive,[5] and at least one other member are appointed by the Treasury. The Bank of England Deputy Governor for prudential regulation is a non-executive member of the board. Two members are appointed jointly by the Secretary of State and the Secretary of the Treasury (non-executive members). The majority of the board members must be non-executive members.

---

3  Financial Services Act 2012 Schedule 1ZB s2.
4  Financial Services Act 2012, Schedule 1ZA s2.
5  The chief executive of the FCA is also a member of the PRA governing body under the Financial Services Act 2012 Schedule 1ZB s3.

## 5.1.2  Regulatory Authority in the US

In the US, the Securities Exchange Commission is the regulatory authority that oversees all securities trading. The SEC is an agency of the US government, established by the Securities Exchange Act of 1934 to 'oversee securities transactions and activities of financial professions with a view to preventing fraud and intentional deception'. The Act empowers the SEC with broad authority over all aspects of the securities industry. The SEC aims to protect investors; maintain fair, orderly, and efficient markets; and facilitate capital formation. Furthermore, it aims to promote a market environment that is worthy of the public's trust.

### 5.1.2.1  Commissioners

The Securities and Exchange Commission has five Commissioners. They are appointed for five years by the President of the United States with the advice and consent of the Senate, but they may serve for an additional 18 months until a replacement is appointed. One of them is named by the President to be the SEC's chief executive.

The SEC contains five divisions and 23 offices. The five divisions are Division of Corporate Finance, Division of Enforcement, Division of Investment Management, Division of Economic and Risk Analysis, and Division of Trading and Markets. The five divisions aim to interpret and enforce securities laws, issue new rules, provide oversight of securities institutions, and coordinate regulation among different levels of government. Furthermore, they monitor US stock exchanges like the New York Stock Exchange and the NASDAQ to ensure that they function properly.

### 5.1.2.2  Power and Authority of SEC

The 1934 Act gives the SEC the power to register, regulate, and oversee brokerage firms, transfer agents, and clearing agencies as well as the nation's securities self-regulatory organisations (SROs), such as the Financial Industry Regulatory Authority (FINRA). Furthermore, the 1934 Act identifies and prohibits certain types of conduct in the markets and provides the Commission with disciplinary powers over regulated entities and persons associated with them.

In addition to the above, the 1934 Act empowers the SEC to require periodic reporting of information by companies with publicly traded securities. For example, companies with more than US$ 10 million in assets whose securities are held by more than 500 owners must file annual and other periodic reports. These reports are available to the public through the SEC's EDGAR database.

The SEC can investigate suspicious financial dealings like insider trading and other forms of financial fraud. It can impose civil penalties, but only has the power to bring civil actions, either in federal courts, district courts, or before an administrative judge (ALJ). The SEC is authorised to take any of the following actions:

1) *Injunctions*: these are orders that prohibit future violations of laws, rules, and regulations. Injunctions are issued in the form of court orders that require a person or company to cease doing something. Failure to comply with an injunction or ignoring an injunction could result in a penalty in the form of a fine or even imprisonment for contempt. There are three kinds of injunctions, namely, temporary restraining orders, preliminary injunctions, and permanent injunctions.

2) *Civil penalties*: one of the most effective sanctions that the SEC can issue is that of civil penalties. It can also order companies to repay any illegal profits it may have made. The plaintiffs in these cases could potentially be awarded 10% to 30% of the total sanctions' proceeds. In practice, the SEC brings many civil enforcement actions against firms and individuals that violate securities laws every year. The SEC is involved in every major case of financial misconduct, either directly or in conjunction with the Justice Department.

3) *Barring or suspension*: the SEC has the power to bar or suspend individuals from acting as corporate officers or directors. Furthermore, it may institute administrative proceedings such as cease and desist orders, revoking or suspending registration, and imposing bars or suspensions of employment.

4) *Appeal*: actions taken by the securities industry's self-regulatory organisations, such as FINRA or the New York Stock Exchange can be appealed to the SEC.

5) *Oversight and regulation*: the scope of the SEC oversight and regulation of securities exchanges and listed companies has increased in both size and complexity, overseen and regulated by the SEC. Until recently, the SEC was charged with overseeing more than 26,000 registered market participants. At present, it oversees 22 national securities exchanges, ten credit rating agencies, and seven active registered clearing agencies. In addition to overseeing the Public Company Accounting Oversight Board, the Financial Industry Regulatory Authority, the Municipal Securities Rulemaking Board, the Securities Investor Protection Corporation, and the Financial Accounting Standards Board, the SEC is also responsible for reviewing the

disclosures and financial statements of almost 4,300 exchange-listed public companies.[6]

### 5.1.3 Regulatory Authority in Kuwait

The Capital Market Authority is the body established to regulate the financial markets in Kuwait. It was founded on the principles of fairness, transparency, and integrity according to the best international practice. Its vision is to work on developing and supervising the activities of capital markets in the State of Kuwait and create an attractive investment environment that obtains investors' trust.[7]

Kuwait classifies its regulatory authorities as independent bodies. In Kuwait, the law states that the authority is an independent body having a legal personality and that it is overseen by the Minister of Trade and Industry.[8] Although the term 'independence' is used, this is not always the case. To that end, the soundness and independence of the regulatory authorities in Kuwait should be assessed in terms of their composition, funding arrangements, accountability, and freedom of action from political and commercial interference.

#### 5.1.3.1 Composition

The regulatory authority is administered by a board called the Board of Commissioners. In Kuwait, the board consists of five full-time members. They are appointed by an Emiri Decree and it specifies the chairman and the deputy chairman.[9] Article 12 mentions that the Emiri Decree determines the board's salaries and benefits.

According to Article 4 of Kuwaiti Law 2010, the Authority's Board of Commissioners shall:

1) Issue necessary bylaws and instructions to execute the Law. It shall also work on issuing recommendations and the necessary studies needed to develop the regulations which assist in achieving its objectives.

6 'The Inspector General's Statement on the SEC's Management and Performance Challenges' (October 2019) www.sec.gov/reports>.
7 <www.cma.gov.kw/en/web/cma/about>.
8 Capital Market Law 2010, Article 2.
9 Capital Market Law 2010, Article 6.

2) With consideration to the provisions of Article (33) of this Law, the Board shall issue licenses to Securities Exchanges and for related activities and shall supervise their activities.

3) Issue licenses to members of Securities Exchanges, and licenses to their employees and anyone who works in the management of securities activities, including asset management and investment funds companies, brokerage companies, securities custody companies, advisory services institutions, etc.

4) Regulate the promotion of investment funds and other Collective Investment Schemes.

5) Regulate Public Subscriptions or Initial Public Offerings (IPOs) and Private Placements for Kuwaiti and non-Kuwaiti Securities and supervise them.

6) Regulate the process of mergers and acquisitions and supervise them.

7) Set up rules of supervision and self-regulatory organisation in securities activities.

8) Approve of the rules and regulations proposed by an Exchange administration prior to commencement of its business.

9) Set up rules for compliance with professional ethics, for competence, and for the integrity of licensed Persons, and approve of the same.

10) Provide appropriate systems to protect Traders and work towards minimizing improper and unfair practices in the securities activities.

11) Cooperate with supervisory authorities and foreign counterpart institutions with regard to organizing, coordinating and participating in joint activities.

12) Carry out all duties and authorities entrusted in it in this Law or any other law with regard to reducing market instability.

13) Issue all necessary decisions which fall within the Authority's competences and are deemed necessary to implement this Law and its Executive Bylaws. It may delegate some of these authorities.

14) Set up special rules, regulations and procedures needed by the licensed Persons who work in accordance with Islamic Sharia.

15) Issue rules for Market Makers.

### 5.1.3.2 Funding Arrangements

In Kuwait, the Authority has an independent budget[10] that does not need to be adopted by the relevant minister. This is because it is not part of the government's general budget and does not need any approval. The

---

10 Capital Market Law 2010, Article 18.

full independence of the regulatory authority budget is resented by some people, who feel that it should be subject to some of the same restrictions as other authorities. An example is discussed in an article published on 10 November 2013 entitled 'Budget War Is Renewed between the Authority and the Ministry of Finance'. The Kuwaiti Ministry of Finance insists that the Authority's budget should be approved by the Minister of Finance, while the Authority asserts that its budget is not subject to such approval.[11]

In Kuwait, the financial resources of the Authority mentioned in Article 19 of the 2010 Law include 1) fees and 2) all other resources that are raised from exercising its activities or recruiting its reserves. Consequently, in Kuwait, there is no funding by the government. The Kuwaiti authorities are allowed to use their reserves.[12] However, this is inconsistent with the text of Article 24, which states that the Authority shall not engage in any commercial activities, lend money, or issue or invest in securities. In comparison, in the UK, the financial services companies, which are regulated, completely fund the FCA. It also has the power to keep sufficient reserves.[13] It does not receive any government funding. However, civil penalties go to the Treasury after deducting the enforcement costs.[14]

### 5.1.3.3  Accountability

In this context, independence does not mean freedom from accountability. The following section addresses to whom a regulatory authority reports.

In the UK, the FCA is an independent body, but it is accountable to the Treasury. For example, the FCA must prepare a report for the Treasury at least once a year, and the Treasury must then submit this report to Parliament.[15]

While some may consider reporting to someone to be different to being overseen by that person, this is not the case in Kuwait. In Kuwait, according to Article 22 of the 2010 Law, the Authority is committed to keeping its accounts and records. In the UK, the FCA is responsible for recording

---

11  <www.alraimedia.com/Articles.aspx?id=464717>.

12  According to Article 4 of the Capital Market Law 2003, the Authority does not allow any of the following four actions: 1) engaging in any commercial activities; 2) acquiring, owning, or issuing securities; 3) lending or borrowing funds; and 4) being part of any project to earn profits.

13  FCA Article 'Power to Raise Fees' <www.fca.org.uk/about/how-we-are-funded/fees>.

14  Financial Services Act 2012, Schedule 1ZA s20.

15  Financial Services Act 2012, Schedule 1ZA s11.

and safekeeping all decisions made in the exercise of its functions,[16] and a record of each governing body meeting must be published.[17] It would be better if Kuwaiti law required the publication of the Authority's meeting reports to achieve transparency. The saying that 'sunshine is the best disinfectant' implies that the publication of the report would avoid any dishonesty.

In conclusion, Kuwaiti law gives the Kuwaiti Capital Market Authority financial and administrative independence, especially with respect to board appointments and its budget and financial resources.

## 5.2 Rule-Making Power

Rules are part of the legal and regulatory framework.[18] This section discusses the advantages and disadvantages of rule-making.

A rule-making authority is an administrative organisation, usually made up of unelected officials, that is charged with implementing policies created by legislation or certain branches of government. It can be described as a discretionary authority as it has the power to decide what course of action to take when implementing existing laws and making rules and enforcing these rules.

As discussed above, the Financial Services Authority is the administrative body tasked with making rules for the securities exchanges and financial services industry in the United Kingdom. In the US, the Securities Exchange Commission and the Financial Industry Regulation Authority perform similar functions of making rules to regulate the securities industry. In Kuwait, this function is performed by the Capital Markets Authority, which is empowered to make rules relating to the listing of securities as well as trading in securities.

Whilst each country has its own legislative process, typically, securities laws are passed by legislative bodies such as parliaments or congress. Rule-making forms part of the general laws and regulations around securities exchanges and the sale of securities. However, rule-making is different in that the rules are passed by an independent administrative body. As such, it is often referred to as secondary legislation.

---

16  Financial Services Act 2012, Schedule 1ZA s9.
17  Ibid s10.
18  Paul Nelson, *Capital Markets Law and Compliance: The Implications of MiFID* (Cambridge University Press 2011) 3–4.

Secondary legislation has advantages:[19]

1) Saving parliamentary time since rules are made without Parliament's involvement. Rules are an alternative to Acts of Parliament. Accordingly, they reduce the statutory burden.[20]
2) Speed, by avoiding the lengthy stages involved in parliamentary procedures. Whilst having the force of law, rules are quicker to pass than a statute.
3) Expertise needed in complicated areas. For example, making rules that regulate the economy requires an understanding of how the economy operates.

Alexander Justham, the former chief executive of the London Stock Exchange, emphasised the importance of rules by saying that 'one of the crucial roles any regulator plays is to examine the marketplace and potentially intervene through rule changes to ensure that an appropriate equilibrium is consistently achieved'.[21]

In addition to these advantages, a regulatory authority can impose civil fines for violations. Whilst both civil and criminal sanctions should be available for effective enforcement,[22] the burden of proof required to impose a criminal sanction is much higher than the burden to impose a civil sanction. Therefore, independent administrative authorities can impose fines as a sanction for violation of its rules in order to enforce these rules.

In 2015, a change was made to Law 2010 Article 146 to allow the Authority to pass civil (administration) penalties, stating that:

> The Disciplinary Board may – after being satisfied that a violation has been committed – issue any of the following penalties: [...] 15 – Imposing financial penalties that are defined according to the severity of the violation not exceeding fifty thousand Kuwait Dinars (KD). In all cases, the Disciplinary Board may cancel all transactions related to the violation and the entailed effects or require the violator to pay amounts equal to the benefit he/she acquired or the value of the loss he/

---

19 <www.lawmentor.co.uk/resources/essays/discuss-advantages-delegated-legislation-form-law-making/>.
20 Paul Nelson (n 151) 20.
21 Article entitled 'New Listing Rules Protect Investors and Safeguard London's Open Markets' (2013) <www.cityam.com/article/1384224375/new-listing-rules-protect-investors-and-safeguard-london-s-open-markets>.
22 Ana Carvajal and Jennifer Elliott, 'The Challenge of Enforcement in Securities Markets: Mission Impossible?' (International Monetary Fund [IMF] working paper 2009) 19.

she has avoided as a result of the violation. The amount may be multiplied if the Person repeats committing the violations.

In 2015, the CMA was granted the authority to fine non-compliant companies or companies that breached the rules. In enforcing its authority in regulating the markets, the CMA issued fines totalling 390,000 KD in the year 2019/2020.[23] Administrative (civil) sanctions differ from criminal fines or sanctions. For example, in Kuwait, the Capital Market Authority must refer to the court to impose criminal sanctions or fines. However, there is a limit of 100,000 KD for criminal fines. This difference can be clearly seen from the case in February 2014 against the Chairman of Al Ahli Bank who traded based on inside information related to the shares of Al Ahli Bank. The first instance court fined him 1.5 million KD, but the appeal court reduced this to 100,000 KD.[24]

The disadvantage of secondary legislation is that delegated rule-making power could have a negative effect in terms of accountability according to the separation of power.[25] Generally, to prevent abuse of power, the executive, legislature, and judiciary's powers should be separate.[26] Rule-making power results in legislation which has not been fully debated in Parliament.[27] Generally, the process of passing a law involves the legislature enacting the law, the executive carrying out the law, and the judiciary resolving disputes about the law. If the law is not clear, judges may interpret the law and, if there is any ambiguity, determine the meaning of the law.[28] Usually, courts will not question a law enacted by Parliament if the law is clear and unambiguous.

However, the situation with secondary legislation is different. The courts are not competent to interpret rules, because they would need to understand the regulatory authority's views, intentions, and policy.[29] Should the secondary legislation exceed its sphere of competence, a court does have the power to strike down the secondary regulation.[30]

---

23  According to the ninth annual report (issued by the Authority) for the year 2019/2020 fines reached within a year about 390,000 KD.
24  <www.reuters.com/article/2014/03/03/ahli-bank-kuwait-court-idUSL6N0M01DK20 140303>.
25  <www.lawteacher.net/free-law-essays/english-legal-system/uk-constitution-excessive -concentration-of-power.php>.
26  <www.essay.uk.com/free-resources/essays/law/constitution-prerogative-powers.php>.
27  Emily Finch and Stefan Fafinski, *English Legal System* (4th edn, Pearson 2013) 11.
28  <http://cw.routledge.com/textbooks/9780415566957/legislation.asp>.
29  Paul Nelson (n 148) 5–6.
30  <www.lawmentor.co.uk/resources/essays/delegated-legislation-controlled-parliament -itself-and-judges-explain-judicial-controls-delegated-legislation/>.

### 5.2.1 *Rule-Making and Regulation in the United Kingdom*

Rule-making is the process by which the FCA and PRA enact rules to supplement existing laws, or to create new rules within existing authority that the agency believes are needed.

### 5.2.2 *Rule-Making and Regulation in the US*

Rule-making is the process by which federal agencies implement legislation passed by Congress and signed into law by the President. In addition, an agency may engage in rule-making to update rules under existing laws, or to create new rules within existing authority that the agency believes are needed.

For the most part, the SEC's authority to issue rules derives from what are generally referred to as the Federal Securities Laws: the Securities Act of 1933, the Securities Exchange Act of 1934, the Investment Company Act of 1940, and the Investment Advisers Act of 1940. Newer laws, such as the Dodd-Frank Wall Street Reform and Consumer Protection Act of 2010, also give rule-making authority and require some specific rule-making by the SEC.

Rule-making generally involves several steps that are designed to give members of the public an opportunity to provide their opinions on whether the agency should reject, approve, or approve with modifications a rule proposal. Here is a brief description of some of these steps:

(i) *Concept release*: the rule-making process usually begins with a rule proposal, but sometimes an issue is so unique or complicated that the SEC seeks public input before issuing a proposed rule. A concept release typically outlines the topic of concern, identifies different potential approaches, and raises a series of questions inviting public comment on the matter. The public's feedback is taken into consideration as the SEC decides which approach, if any, is appropriate.

(ii) *Rule proposal*: when approved by the Commission, a rule proposal is published for public notice and comment for a specified period of time, typically between 30 and 60 days. A rule proposal typically contains the text of the proposed new or amended rule along with a discussion of the issue or problem the proposal is designed to address. The public's input on the proposal is considered as a final rule is drafted.

(iii) *Rule adoption*: when approved by the Commission, the new rule or rule amendment becomes part of the official rules that govern the securities industry. The adopting release reflects the Commission's consideration of the public comments. Many rules are effective immediately, but some have a delayed effective date. In either case, the date by which the public must come into compliance with a new or amended rule (the compliance date) may be delayed or phased in to ensure the transition is a smooth one.

### 5.2.3  Rule-Making and Regulation in Kuwait

In Kuwait, the 2010 Law gives the CMA authority to pass different types of rules. Article 4 of the 2010 Law mentions that:

> [T]he Authority's Board of Commissioners shall:
>
> 1 – Issue necessary bylaws and instructions to execute the Law…
>
> 7 – Set up rules of supervision and self-regulatory organization in Securities activities…
>
> 9 – Set up rules for compliance with professional ethics, for competence, and for the integrity of licensed Persons, and approve of the same…
>
> 13 – Issue all necessary decisions which fall within the Authority's competencies and are deemed necessary to implement this Law and its Executive Bylaws. It may delegate some of these authorities.
>
> 14 – Set up special rules, regulations and procedures needed by the licensed Persons who work in accordance with Islamic Sharia.
>
> 15 – Issue rules for Market Makers.

Rule-making powers are set out under different names such as bylaws, instructions, rules, decisions, special rules, regulations, and procedures.
Article 5 also mentions rule-making power by saying that:

> The Authority shall carry out all the work necessary to achieve its goals, pursuant to this Law, and in particular the following:
>
> 8 – Set up rules to regulate dealing in securities and the transfer of ownership.
>
> 9 – Issue rules to regulate special purpose companies which issue securities.

Whilst it is difficult to set out all types of rules, the most important rules in Kuwait's disclosure rules are listing rules. Furthermore, in Kuwait,[31] a special regulation for securities arbitration was enacted in 2014 through rule-making.

---

31 In Kuwait, article 148 of Law No 7 of 2010 Regarding the Establishment of the Capital Markets Authority and Regulating Securities Activities and its Amendments mentions that 'Disputes arising from the obligations set forth in this Law or any other law if related to transactions of the capital market may be resolved by arbitration, according to such arbitration system as may be adopted by the Authority'.

## 5.3 Listing Rules as an Example of Rule-Making

Before securities can be listed the authorities ensure that disclosure require-ments are met and for the securities to continue to be listed, a complete and exact disclosure of relevant information must be made on a timely basis to facilitate the orderly operation of the stock exchange market.[32]

Listing rules can be described as private law that is binding only as a matter of contract between the listed company (any shareholding company listed on the stock exchange market) and the stock exchange.[33] The part of the listing rules governing disclosure is different from the part stipulating the conditions for listing, which must be satisfied before any shares of a company can be traded on a stock exchange.[34]

There is a difference between listing and public offers. Listing means a regulatory method that makes the securities of a company eligible for trad-ing on a regulated market, while a public offer is an invitation to the public to purchase securities. Listed or unlisted securities can be the subject of a public offer.[35]

History has shown that the conversion of stock exchanges themselves to listed companies in their own right has resulted in a great deal of com-petition for profits. This affects the regulation of stock exchanges and can increase the risk of a regulatory 'race to the bottom' as a result of the con-flicts of interest between the profit of the stock exchange and the responsi-bility to regulate.[36] This development has also led to the rapid development of technology, and the creation of new financial instruments has increased the importance of the stock exchange as a provider, in a competitive market, of specific services, such as trading.[37] Further, today there is international competition between stock exchanges in different countries.[38]

It is important to note that the fewer the companies in the stock market, the lower the profits[39] to the stock exchange. On the other hand, when the listing rules are less stringent, there is the potential to increase the likelihood

---

32 Jonathan Fisher, Jane Bewsey, Malcolm Wayers, and Elizabeth Ovey, *The Law of Investor Protection* (2nd edn, Sweet & Maxwell 2003) 120.
33 Gordon Walker, Terry Reid, Pamela Hanrahan, Ian Ramsay, and Geoff Stapledon, *Commercial Applications of Company Law in New Zealand* (5th edn, CCH 2015) 35.
34 Jonathan Fisher and others (n 162) 119.
35 Iain MacNeil (n 1) 279.
36 Hans Christiansen and Alissa Koldertsova, *The Role Of Stock Exchanges in Corporate Governance* (OECD 2009) 1.
37 Ibid 13.
38 Ibid.
39 According to Article 7 of Resolution No 3 2011, in the Kuwaiti Stock Exchange, the listing companies are required to pay an annual subscription of 0.05% of paid-up capital, not to exceed 50,000 KD.

of damage to the small investors and affect the reputation of the market internationally.

It is important to separate the body that establishes the rules from that which gives permission for listing. In Kuwait, admission to listing and the setting of the rules are controlled by an organisation, the Capital Market Authority, which is separate from the Kuwaiti Stock Exchange. Kuwait Decision No 3 of 2011 sets out listing rules. The first rule is that the Stock Exchange shall not list any company without the approval of the Authority. According to Article 30 of the previous decision No 3, the Kuwaiti legislature has given the Authority the power to refuse any application for listing, if it is not in the best interests of the country.

In the UK, the official list has two segments: the first is the premium (formerly primary) segment, and the second is the standard (formerly secondary) segment. The issuer can apply to either of them. In general, transferring between the two segments can be done without cancelling the issuer's listing but with 20 days' notice to the FSA (now FCA).[40] There are minimum requirements[41] for both segments. These requirements are known as Directive Minimum Standards derived from EU directive standards. However, the premium segment has additional requirements known as super-equivalent standards. The premium segment is only for equity shares.[42] The issuers must have two admissions to be able to trade their securities. The first is admission to listing from the UKLA;[43] the second is admission to trading from the London Stock Exchange[44] (LSE).[45]

---

40  According to LR 5.4A.3 part 3. See also Michael Blair QC, George Walker, and Stuart Willey, *Financial Markets and Exchanges Law* (2nd edn, Oxford University Press 2012) 175–178.

41  That includes validly issued and freely transferable shares, due incorporation and a minimum capitalisation. For example, LR 2.2.7 mentions that 'the expected aggregate market value of all securities to be listed must be at least £700,000 for shares'.

42  Herbert Smith, *A Practical Guide to the UK Listing Regime* (2nd edn, ICSA 2011) 48–49.

43  The UKLA is one of the FCA divisions. It is responsible for regulation of the granting of right to securities listed in the official List (premium or standard segment).

44  The LSE has market rules with which companies must comply, such as Rule 1.8, which requires the listed company to have a contact person who is responsible for ongoing disclosure and to inform the LSE of any change in this person; Herbert Smith (n 172) 35.

45  <www.londonstockexchange.com/companies-and-advisors/main market/companies/listing/process.htm>.

# 6    Disclosure of Inside Information

In the conduct of its business, a company is required to disclose several kinds of information. Information relating to its financial position is disclosed in periodic reporting (annual and half-yearly reports). Additionally, information related to the business list of assets is declared, especially notification of the acquisition or disposal of major shareholdings, or acquisition or disposal of any fixed assets of the listed company. Furthermore, information such as notification of transactions by persons discharging managerial responsibilities (disclosure of dealing) are needed by investors to make informed decisions about whether to buy or sell their shares in the company.

All this information is available in the public domain and has a direct impact on the share price of a company. Inside information, however, is information that is not yet public, but that will have an impact on the share price of the company. People who deal based on this kind of information before it becomes public are in a better position to buy or sell shares in a company than those people who are not aware of it. For this reason, dealing in insider information is wrong and is criminalised in most legal systems.

It is important to understand the term 'inside information'. It refers to specific information related to the company which, if published, would be likely to have a significant effect on the share price. It is a piece of key information that makes individual investors aware of fundamental benefits and risks when making an investment decision (buying, selling, or deferring investment). Disclosure of inside information should be accurate, honest, understandable, full, timely, and not misleading.

Some say that 'informed investors are protected investors'.[1] Disclosure is intended to empower investors and give them the opportunity to make an

---

1 John T A Burke, 'Re-examining Investor Protection in Europe and the US' [2009] 16(2) *eLaw Journal: Murdoch University Electronic Journal of Law* 10.
<http://elaw.murdoch.edu.au/index.php/elawmurdoch/article/viewFile/38/13>.

DOI: 10.4324/9781003301875-7

informed decision. There must also be a suitable mechanism for implementing and enforcing them.[2] In the UK, several mechanisms exist, namely, the listing principles, director responsibilities, the insider list, the reasonable investor standard, the adviser, and holiday disclosures, which are similar in the Kuwait regime.

The disclosure of inside information by listed companies is one of the most important objectives of the Kuwait securities market. For instance, the Kuwait legislation stresses the importance of disclosure of information in accordance with the provision of Article 3 of Kuwaiti Law No 7 of 2010, which says that one of the Kuwaiti Capital Market Authority's objectives is 'implementation of a policy of full disclosure to achieve justice, transparency and prevent conflicts of interest and the exploitation of inside information'.

## 6.1  The Regulatory Framework for Disclosure

There are four types of laws and rules that make up the framework for disclosure.

1. *Listing rules*: these impose a continuing obligation on listed companies to disclose meaningful information.
2. *Disclosure rules*: the UK and Kuwait have specific rules for disclosure.
3. *Market abuse rules*: these aim to eliminate insider trading, manipulation, and misleading disclosure.
4. *Criminal offences*: there are various criminal offences associated with disclosure.

These rules have the potential to provide better protection for investors by ensuring that the market operates on the basis of equal access and fair disclosure of inside information and by ensuring that the disclosure does not mislead investors' decisions.

## 6.2  What Is Disclosure of Inside Information?

The definition of 'inside information' varies from country to country. Kuwaiti legislation provides approximately 25 examples of inside information, after which it gives a general standard for determining it.

---

2 Niamh Moloney, *How to Protect Investors: Lessons from the EC and the UK* (CUP 2010) 300–301.

For the purposes of this section, disclosure of inside information means:

> Full, timely, and accurate disclosure of information about a listed company's activities to provide equal opportunities for investment and to promote investor confidence and market integrity.

Therefore, issuers[3] are required to provide investors with information that could affect their investment decisions, because such information can affect the prices of securities. The FSA (now FCA) Director of Enforcement and Financial Crime, Tracey McDermott, stated, 'The integrity of our markets depends on listed companies making timely and accurate disclosures'.[4] Examples of inside information that needs to be disclosed are material events, major changes in company policies, and decisions related to a major investment or capital purchase.

Ensuring that investors are sufficiently informed is one of the reasons for the regulatory intervention in financial markets that could help an investor to make a suitable investment assessment. The former director of the FSA (now FCA) Alexander Justham, stated, 'JJB's failure to disclose information… denied investors the ability to fully understand its financial position and make informed investment decisions'.[5] If the market fails to protect investors from making bad decisions because of inadequate or incomplete information, and if, as a result, investors lose confidence in the market, investors will withdraw from the market forever, and the market will suffer from reduced liquidity.[6]

### 6.2.1 Rules about Disclosure of Information in the UK

In the UK, the disclosure should be made as soon as possible, and there should be legitimate reasons for any delay in making the disclosure. Therefore, it is unacceptable to delay the announcement because of a delay in obtaining approval from the board because the company is preparing the announcement, or because the presentation to analysts is not ready.[7] A timely disclosure is important even though a listed company feels that delaying the disclosure will reduce its impact.

---

3 According to Article 1 of the Kuwaiti Disclosure Rules 2/2012, the issuer means a legal person (legal entity) whose security has been listed on a stock market.
4 FSA/PN/024/2013; an enforcement decision was taken by the FSA.
5 FSA/PN/015/2011; an enforcement decision was taken by the FSA against JJB Sports PLC, which was fined £455,000 for failing to disclose information to the market.
6 Brian McDonnell, A Practitioner's Guide to Inside Information (2nd edn, Sweet & Maxwell 2012) 3.
7 'Technical Note: Disclosure and Transparency Rules: UKLA' (Financial Services Authority) 4; it is not binding. It serves as an explanation.

Assessing what constitutes inside information is not straightforward, because it depends on different factors, such as changes in the issuer's business, operations, and capital. The issuer is in the best position to determine whether inside information exists that could significantly affect securities prices. Therefore, the best solution for controlling the disclosure of inside information is to make an issuer responsible for a disclosure in a way that can be clearly seen from the listing principles in the UK, which mentions that adequate procedures, systems, and controls must be established by an issuer (listing principle two) to comply with its obligations.

### 6.2.2 Rules about Disclosure of Information in the US

Congress has empowered the SEC to create and revise its own rules that are applied to the securities industry. What follows is a brief discussion of the most important rules made by the SEC relating to the disclosure of information.

(i)  *Rule 10b-5* was created by the SEC under section 10(b) of the Securities Exchange Act of 1934. It states:

> It shall be unlawful for any person, directly or indirectly, by the use of any means or instrumentality of interstate commerce, or of the mails or of any facility of any national Securities exchange, (a) to employ any device, scheme, or artifice to defraud, (b) to make any untrue statement of a material fact or to omit to state a material fact necessary in order to make the statements made, in the light of the circumstances under which they were made, not misleading, or (c) to engage in any act, practice, or course of business which operates or would operate as a fraud or deceit upon any person, in connection with the purchase or sale of any security.

(ii)  *Rule 408.* Companies are required to disclose any 'further material information, if any, as may be necessary to make the required statements in light of the circumstances under which they were made not misleading'.

(iii)  *Rule 12b-20.* In addition, rule 12b-20 requires adding such further material information, if any, as may be necessary to make the required statements, in the light of the circumstances under which they are made, not misleading.

As can be seen from these rules, the SEC gives special attention to the truthfulness and trustworthiness of information that is provided to others by players in the industry.

There is great debate about whether these rules or the efficient capital market hypothesis (ECMH) are enough. The latter hypothesis states that in an efficient market, present prices always and fully reflect all relevant information about securities being traded. Therefore, there is a relationship between information and the price of a security in an efficient market.

After the stock market crash of 1929 and the Great Depression that followed, the Federal Securities Law was established to make it compulsory for companies to give full disclosure to potential investors.

Securities regulation is mandatory due to the fact that in securities markets there is no observable product quality or asymmetrical information that investors could use to determine the value of the particular security. It is, therefore, vital that true and trustworthy information be disclosed to the market, including the following categories of information:

(i) *Financials*: past financial documents are a good indication of the company's performance over a period of time. They also assist investors to compare how the company is doing at present when compared with its past performance.

(ii) *Management*: who are the members of the management team? How much experience do they have? How are they compensated?

(iii) *Business*: information relating to technology used by the business and any costs associated with using this technology is extremely important. It is also vital to know how the business uses this technology to improve its business and attract customers.

(iv) *Industry*: investors are interested in knowing the current state of the industry that the business trades in. Of particular interest would be the details surrounding competition and potential new developments that could affect the business. Any other threats or opportunities presented by the industry would be relevant.

(v) *Regulation*: regulation by the state or federal government has the potential to affect the business, especially the costs of doing business. Current regulations and potential future regulations need to be disclosed, as well as the cost implication of these for the business.

(vi) *Risk*: what is the beta for other companies in similar industries.

It is important to have:

(i) *Transparency*: all information provided should be accurate and relevant to ensure that potential investors are able to make educated decisions related to investing in the business.

(ii) *Information*: all information should be timely and up to date and businesses need to make full disclosure of all potential strengths and weaknesses that could affect the business.

(iii) *Market fragmentation*: investors need to be informed about any fragmentation in the market or industry as this has the effect of increasing
volatility in the industry and can, thus, affect the business' profitability
and stability.
(iv) *Fraud*: all cases of fraud need to be brought to light, particularly as
investors need to be assured that cases of fraud will not be covered up
and action will be taken against the perpetrators of such crimes.

Full disclosure is seen as a positive development as it can impact managers'
behaviour. Managers may be tempted to maximise their own personal wel-
fare at the expense of shareholders' interests. However, when all relevant
information is disclosed, shareholders can hold managers to account for
such behaviour.

### 6.2.3 *Rules about Disclosure of Information in Kuwait*

The basic statutory framework for disclosure relating to securities in Kuwait
is set out in the Capital Market Law and two rules: Rule No 3 of 2011, relating to listing, and Rule No 2 of 2012, relating to disclosure.

The Capital Market Law makes provision for a number of crimes related
to the disclosure process. Article 119 states that a person may be imprisoned
'if he/she has been found to have obtained in any manner a benefit, interest or consideration for himself/herself or for others in consideration of the
disclosure of a secret or piece of information'.

Furthermore, Article 120 provides for a fine if

> any Person who omits, conceals, or prevents information with material
> effect – that the Law or the Bylaws require to be provided or disclosed
> to the Authority or an Exchange – in connection with the purchase or
> sale of a Security or in connection with a recommendation to purchase
> or sell a Security.

In addition to the Capital Market Law, there are rules issued by the Capital
Market Authority relating to disclosure.

'Disclosure' and 'transparency' are two terms that go hand in hand, as
each relates to information. It should be noted here that the bylaw has put
in place a special code, under the title 'Disclosure and Transparency', to
oblige companies to disclose and be transparent with certain information.
This leads to a heavy burden on companies who are obliged to abide by
these rules which are repeated in the fifteenth code (governance, which is
the tenth code for companies).

The rule of 'accurate and timely disclosure and transparency' is of great importance. The executive regulations of the Capital Markets Authority Law 2010 deal with this in detail. Accordingly, there may be common points between the rules of governance and other rules such as the rules of exclusion and transparency, and a penalty may be issued for violating any of these rules.

An example of the application of these rules is cases numbers 95 and 96/2019 Disciplinary Board, 27 and 28/2019 complaint filed against Arshid AZM Al-Houri, in his capacity as the Chairman of the Board of Directors of YIACO Medical Company, in which the Capital Markets Authority announced that he had violated Circulars 7 and 12 of 2017, and the provisions of Article 1-6-1 of Module Ten (Disclosure and Transparency), and Articles 8-1, 8-2, and 8-4 of the previous rule (Ensure Timely and High-Quality Disclosure and Transparency) of Module 15 (Corporate Governance) of the Executive Bylaws of Law No 7 of 2010 Regarding the Establishment of the Capital Markets Authority. Therefore, the following resolution was issued:

> First: Imposing a fine on the violator with an amount of KWD 3,000 for the violations committed. The violator did not obtain CMA's approval for reducing the capital of YIACO Medical Company. Second: Cancelling the voting clause on the Company's capital reduction passed during the extraordinary general assembly on 17-10-2019 with its consequent implications.[8]

As can be seen from this case, the CMA is quick to exercise its authority in implementing the rules and laws relating to accurate and timely disclosure and transparency.

### 6.2.4 *Difficulties Related to Disclosure*

There are several criticisms of the system of disclosure of inside information which affect competition because early disclosure can reveal the company's plans and future projects to a competitor in the market. In addition, in practice, there is difficulty in identifying inside information because of the lack of an accurate standard and because issuers can differ in their understanding of fundamental information.

It is a difficult challenge to identify material (inside) information and to determine the appropriate time to announce it. For example, in Kuwait,

---

8 Abdullah Alshebbli, *Legal Framework for Corporate Governance on the Kuwaiti Stock Exchange* (Academic Publication Concile 2021) 118.

a seminar organised by the Kuwaiti Capital Markets Authority (KCMA) related to the disclosure of inside information was attended by many legal advisers of listed companies and compliance managers from the Authority. Several participants in the seminar expressed dissatisfaction because of the many grey areas contained in the answers given by the Authority officials present. The KCMA officials stressed the need for the immediate disclosure of inside information. This was the subject of controversy when the audience asked about one of the criteria that determined what information is material. The Authority replied that this is determined by the issuers. Every piece of information that has an impact on the financial position is essential. Commission officials stressed that any information that can lead to a change in the share price and trading volumes requires disclosure, even if it is secret or if the company is in the process of completing some of the agreements; for example, if a company has signed a confidentiality agreement to restructure or study something with any of the consulting houses. The officials emphasised the need to disclose to the Commission and the Stock Exchange before publishing the announcement in the newspapers and the media in general or on the company's website. One member of the audience complained that the Authority laid down harsh sanctions despite having failed to set accurate and clear standards to identify inside information. One attendee expressed dismay, because these requirements, which require revealing to a competitor important information about pricing and secrets about the other company, may prove unfair to listed companies as most of their competitors are not listed on the Stock Exchange.[9] Hence, this is a disadvantage of listing.

## 6.3  Disclosure Principles

There are many principles that are applicable to the issue of disclosure The following section will discuss these principles in more detail.

### 6.3.1  Delay and Extent of Disclosure

Companies can delay their public disclosure of inside information if a number of conditions are met in certain circumstances. Disclosure may be delayed to protect the legitimate interest of the company, if it is not misleading to the public, or if a duty of confidentiality is owed to the issuer by whoever is receiving the inside information, and confidentiality is ensured by the issuer.

---

9  <www.alqabas.com.kw/node/735010>.

In Kuwait, if inside information is delayed due to ongoing negotiations that have not yet been resolved, or if there are contracts or agreements requiring accreditation from another party to become effective, an issuer has the right to request a delay of disclosure from the KCMA, if there is no possibility of misleading the public and there is a guarantee from the issuer that the inside information will remain confidential.[10] There is no evidence on whether this request is usually granted or not.

### 6.3.2 Limited Disclosure

Disclosure can be limited in certain circumstances. In the UK, companies can disclose inside information to a person who owes a confidential duty to the issuer provided that other conditions are also met such as not breaching other laws and regulations. However, it is unacceptable to disclose inside information to journalists, for example, because they do not have a duty of confidentiality to the issuer.[11]

### 6.3.3 Initial and Final Disclosure

If a serious and unexpected event occurs, and the company needs more time to understand the situation before making a disclosure, it can apply to the regulatory authorities for a temporary halt in trading or make an initial disclosure to be followed later by a full disclosure.

### 6.3.4 Dealing with Rumours

The greater the delay in disclosure of the correct information the higher the risk of rumours. The disclosure rules also deal with rumours and false information which may arise as a result of a delay in disclosing the correct information.

In Kuwait, an issuer should immediately clarify, confirm, or deny, without any delay, when there is speculation, news, or current information related to the issuer's shares that is likely to affect the prices of its securities or is linked to the investment decisions of traders, regardless of whether the information is true or false.[12] Here, if the unusual trading does not stop, the Kuwait Authority has the right to impose a temporary suspension of trading.

---

10 Kuwaiti Disclosure Rules 2012 Article 5.
11 Technical note (n 182) 8.
12 Kuwait Disclosure Rules 2/2012 Article 6.

Sometimes, people may take advantage of a rumour that is the result of the lack of clear disclosure or of leaks. This can cause unusual trading activity. For example, in Kuwait, if unusual trading occurs the issuer must take one of the following actions:

a)  Re-disclose inside information if the issuer determines that it happened as a result of a previous disclosure.
b)  Consult with the Authority if an issuer believes that it happened as a result of the absence of interpretation or a misunderstanding.
c)  Comment immediately without delay if there are rumours.
d)  Disclose inside information if there are leaks of information.
e)  Make a general announcement, including that nothing new has happened, if the issuer does not find the reason for the unusual trading.

Therefore, the Authority could apply a temporary suspension if the issuer could not remedy the unusual trading.[13]

### 6.3.5  *Directors' Responsibilities for Controlling Disclosure*

There are two important points concerning how to control inside information. The first is how to determine that the information is inside information. The second is how to establish a suitable time for the disclosure. Making a limited group from the board of directors responsible for releasing inside information to the public could improve the situation and could make it highly susceptible to control.

In the UK, Listing Rule 9.2.11R mentions 'the contact person', which means at least one suitable person (with knowledge about the company) who updates the contact with the FCA and whom the issuer must nominate as the first point of contact with the FCA regarding listing rules and DTRs.

Article 1.3.2 of the Executive Bylaws 2015 mentions that:

> Each Listed Company shall assign a Person to be responsible for responding to the Authority's questions concerning disclosure and transparency.

### 6.3.6  *Insiders' Lists*

In the UK, the issuer must provide the FCA with an insider list detailing the persons who have access to inside information (DTR 2.8). The issuer must

---

13 Kuwait Disclosure Rules 2/2012 Article 6.

keep this list ready and when the FCA requests it, the issuer must provide this list as soon as possible. In the UK, 'as soon as possible' means without delay.[14]

In Kuwait, Article 3.5.1 of the Executive Bylaws 2015 mentions that 'A Listed Company shall prepare a list of its Insiders'.

Having an insider list is better than preventing directors and senior executives from trading. Although both would achieve the same goal, the latter is more restrictive and less effective.

### 6.3.7  An Adviser

An issuer can use an appropriate adviser to consult about any information, especially to know whether the information reaches the level of inside information. Companies cannot rely on the adviser's opinion to determine whether information needs to be disclosed.

Kuwait has no mention in its rules regarding how to use an appropriate adviser to consult about any information.

### 6.3.8  The Reasonable Investor Standard

An issuer must consider the reasonable investor standard when determining whether the information is price sensitive; in other words, whether the investment decision of a reasonable investor would be significantly affected by undisclosed information if it were made public knowledge. This evaluation is different from one issuer to another because it depends on different factors, such as the sector, the issuer's activities, and the reliability of the sources of information.[15]

Kuwaiti disclosure rules 2/2012 have chosen a 'prudent person standard' to determine inside information. The standard is defined as 'a person who seeks to maximise his benefits if he can use the inside information when making his investment decisions'. Disclosure rules emphasise that a prudent person standard varies from one investor to another depending on several factors, such as the issuer's size, recent developments, the general situation of the market, and, in particular, the issuer's sector.

14  Michael Blair QC, George Walker, and Stuart Willey (n 170) 198.
15  Louise Wolfson (Continuing Obligations: A Practitioner's Guide to the Financial Services Authority Listing Regime 2012/2013 (25th edn, Thompson Reuters 2012) 228.

### 6.3.9  Weekend Disclosure

During the weekend, the UK stock exchanges are closed. Therefore, special provisions are needed to deal with this. In the UK, there is what is known as the 'Friday Night Drop' case. The name comes from the fact that when a Regulatory Information Service (RIS)[16] is closed on Friday evening, the permitted delay in disclosure to the authorities is until the RISs reopen on Monday morning. However, over the weekend the information must be made public by the company in one newspaper.[17] This situation is not clear in Kuwait.

### 6.3.10  Form of the Disclosure

A written announcement helps to explain the information and to provide clarity. Kuwaiti laws do not require a special method of disclosure. In the UK, regulatory disclosure must be written.[18]

---

16  RISs are the places that must disseminate inside information on behalf of listed companies after receiving the information on the full text of the regulatory disclosure, and after the disclosure has been approved by the FSA.

17  Technical note (n 182) 8.

18  Technical note (n 182) 2.

# 7 Securities Crimes

Securities crimes are offences that relate to deceptive practices in the stock or commodities markets. They are primarily aimed at getting investors to purchase or sell securities on the basis of false information, frequently resulting in losses. The most common securities crimes are manipulation and insider dealing. Securities crime is defined as 'illegal or unethical activity carried out involving securities or asset markets in order to profit at the expense of others'. Securities crimes can be committed in a variety of forms but typically involve misrepresenting information investors use to make decisions or affecting the prices of the stocks or commodities.

The perpetrator of a securities crime is usually an individual, such as a stockbroker. However, it can be an organisation, such as a brokerage firm, corporation, or investment bank. Independent individuals might also commit this type of crime through schemes such as insider trading. Examples of securities crimes include Ponzi schemes, pyramid schemes, and late-day trading. Offences can also include false information, pump-and-dump schemes, or trading on insider information, which includes providing false information, withholding key information, offering bad advice, and offering or acting on inside information.

Securities crimes take on many forms. In fact, there is no shortage of methods used to trick investors with false information. High-yield investment fraud, for example, may come with guarantees of high rates of return while claiming there is little to no risk. The investments themselves may be in commodities, securities, real estate, and other categories. Advance fee schemes can follow a more subtle strategy, where the fraudster convinces their targets to advance them small amounts of money that are promised to result in greater returns.

Whilst there are many types of securities crimes, this chapter will focus on manipulation and insider dealing as these are the most common in practice.

DOI: 10.4324/9781003301875-8

## 7.1 Manipulation

Manipulation or illegal speculation is one of the oldest illegal acts that takes place in securities markets. Speculating on the price of certain commodities is part of the process of dealing in securities and is supported by the community, contributing to the development of the economy and the prosperity of securities markets. However, manipulation occurs when traders use information or other means at their disposal to cause an increase in the price (in their favour) or decrease in the price of stocks or commodities. This type of speculation is illegal and harms the securities market and society.[1]

In recent times, there has been a continuous increase in public awareness with regard to the importance of regulating market manipulation and investigating manipulation. Manipulation of stock prices, lying on SEC filings, and committing accounting fraud are particular types of securities fraud. Some famous examples of this are the Enron, Tyco, Adelphia, and WorldCom scandals. The term market manipulation refers to a type of market abuse where there is a deliberate attempt to interfere with the free and fair operation of the market by creating artificial, false, or misleading appearances with respect to the price of, or market for, a product, security, commodity, or currency. Manipulation is one form of market abuse. Other forms include insider dealing and misleading the market.

In Kuwait, market manipulation practices came under regulation for the first time through Law No 7 in 2010. Previously, regulation of market manipulation practices was almost non-existent. Law No 7 of 2010 does not use the term 'market manipulation' or even define it. However, it mentions the forms of manipulative practices encompassed by the law.

In general, the prices of securities or commodities are determined by supply and demand and other relevant market factors. A security's price reflects all known information. However, manipulation occurs when the quality of information available in the market is designed to affect the prices of securities or commodities. This has the effect of driving the price of the security or commodity up or down to an artificial level, creating artificial prices. The intent of the person spreading the false information is to induce others to trade and then to profit from these trades or the effects of the trades. Market manipulation is harmful to traders and can put the market at a higher risk of collapse.

Manipulation of the information reduces market efficiency. Sometimes, the supply and demand principle is hampered by the artificial transactions

---

1 Abdullah Alshebli, 'Manipulation in Stock Exchange' (Master Thesis Submitted to Kuwait University, 2008) 40.

of market manipulation. This could lead to the creation of false information, fictitious trades, and fake prices. Manipulation weakens traders' confidence in the market. Most countries do not have sufficiently clear laws relating to the definition of manipulation but do set out to name specific instances of it.

The most common market manipulation forms can be divided into three categories: 1) manipulation based on information, 2) manipulation based on artificial transactions, and 3) price manipulation. In the UK, market manipulation is regulated under the FSMA 2000 sections 118 and 397. The words 'market manipulation' have been described as 'a term of art' by the US Supreme Court.[2] In Kuwait, the legislature attempted to define manipulation in Law No 7 of 2010. Article 22 of this law mentions that:

> A punishment by imprisonment for a term of not more than five years and fine of not less than ten thousand Dinars and not more than one hundred thousand Dinars, or by either of these two penalties, shall be incurred by any Person who is proved to have intentionally committed one of the following acts:

1) Behaves in a way that creates a false impression or misleads people concerning the actual trading in a security or a Security Exchange through:
   a) Entering into a deal in a manner that is not conducive to real change in the security's ownership;
   b) Entering a purchase or sale order for a security with the knowledge that a similar order in terms of size, price, time of sale or purchase for the same security, has been or will be issued by the same Person or by Persons who act in agreement with that Person.
2) Whoever concludes one or more deals concerning a security, that would lead to:
   a) An increase in the price of the security for the purpose of encouraging others to purchase it.
   b) A reduction in the price of the security for the purpose of encouraging others to sell it.
   c) Creating actual or fictitious trading for the purpose of encouraging others to purchase or sell. The Authority shall set the rules explaining the instances included in Clause (1/a) and Clause (2/c). Such rules shall specify practices to be exempted from the implementation of the provision of this Article.

---

2 *Santa Fe Industries Inc v Green* (1977) 430 US 462, 477.

Most countries have a clear definition of the concept of manipulation. However, their efforts at enforcing these laws have proved to be lacking. Enforcement and investigation of manipulation are extremely important, as, without enforcement of the law, traders will continue to use manipulation to affect the markets. In Kuwait, Law No 7 of 2010 aims to curb market manipulation. It is a good first step towards stopping it. However, it would not be effective to end manipulative practices without efficient enforcement.[3]

Whilst Kuwaiti law makes manipulation a crime, there are some people who argue that manipulation should not be criminalised. A clear example of this is set out in a case brought before the Constitutional Court in 2014.[4] The Court decided to reject the argument that manipulation should be allowed. In this case, the claimant argued that there was no clear definition of what constitutes manipulation and, furthermore, that it was against the constitutional provisions relating to personal freedom. The claimant argued that:

> The Act 2010 did not define (article 122) clearly, accurately, and unambiguously, and the wording of its phrases were loose, very broad and comprehensive. These acts [manipulation] vary among themselves in terms of their weight and their seriousness, which necessitates with them a gradual punishment in a manner that would achieve proportionality and balance between the punishment and the crime. In addition, the fact that some of these acts do not necessarily require the determination of a criminal punishment when they are committed, makes this provision suspicious of contradiction with the text of Articles (30) and (32) of the Constitution.

The court rejected these arguments and ruled that Article 122 made it clear what the crime of manipulation is.

Whilst Article 30 of the Constitution does afford people the right of personal freedom, this can be limited on the basis of law. In this regard, Article 32 of the Constitution states that 'There is no crime and no punishment except on the basis of a law'. Thus, the legislator has the duty to establish crimes and determine the penalties that suit them, even if these encroach on certain freedoms. In this case, the court stated that personal freedom, as set out in Article 30 of the Constitution, can be limited in line with Article 32 of the Constitution. However, for personal freedom to be limited, it is

---

3 Fatemah Abdulla Al Shuraian, 'Market Manipulation in Kuwait Stock Exchange: An Analysis of the Regulation of Market Manipulation Prior and Under Law No 7 of 2010' (Thesis submitted for the degree of Doctor of Philosophy at the University of Leicester) 250.
4 Case No 41 of 2014.

imperative that the wrongful acts must be categorically defined in a way that prevents them from being confused with others.

The court ruled that Article 122 was sufficiently clear and not unconstitutional. The goal of the Article is to protect those who trade in capital markets by curbing illegal, inappropriate, and unfair practices. The legislator criminalised manipulation because it disrupts the trading in the markets and negatively affects the confidence of those who are involved in such markets. The Article makes it clear what actions should be avoided to escape the punishment as set out in the law. Furthermore, the law acts as a general deterrent to others to refrain from committing the crime.

### 7.1.1 Ponzi Schemes

A Ponzi scheme can be described as a form of manipulation where the perpetrator convinces investors to invest money in a particular fund on the promise of high returns on their investment. Typically, the perpetrator pays the investor the return promised either from the capital invested or from amounts paid to him by other investors. By attracting more and more investors, the perpetrator can continue paying the original investors the promised returns, from the capital invested by the new investors. However, these schemes are destined to collapse on themselves as the amounts being paid out exceed those being invested. These schemes are used by brokers or other professionals who become rich from the fees and other charges levied against the invested monies.

### 7.1.2 Pump-and-Dump

A pump-and-dump scheme consists of the manipulation of a stock price by means of fraudulent information. Typically, the perpetrator will spread false information that leads to an increase in the price of the stock. These bad actors try to manipulate the stock for their own advantage by buying a stock at a low price. Once the stock reaches a significantly high enough price, the perpetrator dumps or sells the stock he owns. However, usually, the fraudulent information is exposed and the inflated price of the stock tumbles, leading to losses for those who relied on the false information.

This type of scheme uses internet chat rooms or social media including WhatsApp groups and forums to spread the false or fraudulent information. In the past, a pump-and-dump scheme was often initiated by using a 'wrong number' scam. A message is left on victims' answering machines talking of a hot stock tip and is constructed so that the victim would think that the message was an accident. The intention is to force a price increase in those stocks – the pump, and then once the price reaches a certain level, sell them off – the dump.

## 7.2  Insider Trading

Insider trading involves trading in a public company's stock by someone who has non-public, material information about that stock for any reason. Insider trading can be either illegal or legal depending on when the insider makes the trade. It is illegal when the material information is still non-public, and this sort of insider trading comes with harsh consequences.

Material non-public information is any information that could substantially impact an investor's decision to buy or sell the security that has not been made available to the public. This form of insider trading is illegal and comes with stern penalties including both potential fines and jail time. However, insider trading can be legal if it conforms to the rules set forth by the Capital Market Authority.

There is no doubt that information is particularly important when buying or selling in the stock market because information can materially affect the value of the securities. But, if access to information is limited to a group according to their positions, without which they cannot obtain the information, other investors will lose the opportunity to make a profit. Insider dealing adversely affects the opportunity that should be available to everyone in the market to have open access to information. This is known as the 'principle of equality' of having simultaneous access to information.[5] Since investors depend on information to make good decisions at the right and appropriate time, a problem arises when only some investors know the positive or negative information, which can lead to shortcomings in the principle of equal access.

Decisions on whether to buy or sell are based on information collected from the market. The problem arises, however, when the information comes from confidential sources, and only a few people have access to it. This leads to the violation and derogation of the fairness of the market because of the inequality created by their position or their relationship to the source of the information.

Promoting investor confidence in securities markets and, in particular, ensuring that those participating in the markets do so on the same informational footing is one of the goals of the capital market worldwide. This goal cannot be achieved without regulating insider dealing.

---

5 Article 3 of Executive Regulations of Kuwaiti Law No 7 of 2010 provides that 'The Authority aims to: 1. Organise the Securities business in line with the principles of equity, efficiency, competitiveness and transparency'.

### 7.2.1 Background to Insider Dealing

Insider dealing is not a recent phenomenon. It has a long history, and most countries have a special way to combat and fight it. An increasing number of countries prohibit insider dealing by law. Even so, debate over the control of insider dealing has continued since the 1960s, and countries have different experiences with, and responses to, insider dealing. For example, the first judicial decision banning insider dealing was handed down in the United States in the case of *Re Cady, Roberts & Co.*[6]

Whilst almost every stock exchange market bans insider dealing, they differ in the manner of addressing it. The two large competing markets, the European Union (EU) including the UK and the United States, have different systems for combating insider dealing. The EU recognises a breach of the duty of fairness to the market and other uninformed investors by using insider information obtained from a person in possession. The United States recognises insider dealing to be a violation of fiduciary duties or breaching a duty of confidence owed to the source of information.[7]

When considering insider dealing, it is helpful to focus on the United States as it has a long history and extensive experience in this regard.[8] The United States, which is the home of the world's largest capital market, was one of the first jurisdictions to make insider trading illegal.[9] There is a vast amount of information regarding the detection and prosecution of insider dealing under American law. Stephen Bainbridge, UCLA law professor and noted author, said that 'prohibition of insider trading will reward study not only for USA corporate and securities law scholars, but those of all countries'.[10] However, Bainbridge describes the modern American securities regulation as a complex, federally imposed ban of insider dealing and this is a central feature of the regulations.[11]

---

6 40 SEC 907 (1961). In *Cady, Roberts & Co* a board member had given important information about an imminent dividend cut in a firm to a stockbroker, as a result of which the broker sold the company's shares. In 1961, the Disclose or Abstain Rule was established by this case.

7 Ibid 2.

8 Stephen Bainbridge, 'Insider Trading' in Stephen Bainbridge (ed), *Insider Trading* (Edward Elgar 2011) 700.

9 Stephen Bainbridge, *An Overview of Insider Trading Law and Policy: An Introduction to the Insider Trading Research Handbook* 2013 2. <http://ssrn.com/abstract=2141457>.

10 Ibid 2.

11 Ibid 3.

### 7.2.2  *Definition of Insider Dealing*

Generally, insider dealing involves trading (selling or buying) in a specific company's securities by a person linked to that company, who, by virtue of that link, has inside information that would change the securities' price if this information were made public knowledge.[12] Such a person who possesses inside information could not achieve any profit from the trade if they did not have the link to the company.

Bainbridge defines insider dealing as 'trading in securities while in possession of material non-public information'.[13] This can be illustrated by the following example. A director of a company, who learns of good or bad news during a board meeting, buys or sells the company's shares to profit from the undisclosed information before the information is disclosed to the public. Under such circumstances, the director is involved in insider dealing. In this example, the director is seeking to take advantage of his position inside a company. This is also an example of the misuse of confidential data.

Insider dealing also includes a situation where a person with confidential information persuades another person to trade in securities. Furthermore, insider dealing occurs when a person avoids a loss or makes a profit by misusing confidential information gained through the person's position within the company.[14]

It should be underlined that the key to passing effective legislation against insider dealing is to define it properly. The definition must cover the following four areas:

- Who is an insider?
- What is the inside information?
- How is the inside information transferred?
- What action is banned?

### 7.2.2.1  *Who Is an Insider?*

In the past, 'insiders' were divided into two categories: primary insiders and secondary insiders. Primary insiders may hold such positions as members of the board of directors, managers, in-house accountants, and in-house lawyers, among others. These people hold positions that enable them to obtain information through the company's management or supervision.

---

12  Gill Brazier, *Insider Dealing: Law & Regulation* (Cavendish Publishing Limited 1996) 76.
13  Stephen Bainbridge, *Insider* (n 201) 701.
14  Barry Rider, Kern Alexander, and Lisa Linklater, *Market Abuse and Insider Dealing* (Butterworths Compliance Series LexisNexis 2002) 4.

Alternatively, secondary insiders are those who receive information directly or indirectly with full knowledge of the importance of the inside information through primary insiders.[15] This includes people who work with the company through their profession, such as external accountants and lawyers.

Today, much of the legislation defines insiders differently in that it does not distinguish between primary and secondary insiders. For example, the UK defines an insider as any person who has inside information (he knows it is inside information) from an inside source (he knows that he has obtained it from an inside source) according to section 57 of the Criminal Justice Act (CJA) 1993.

### 7.2.2.2 What Is Inside Information?

Before defining inside information, the value of information in the financial market should be appreciated to understand insider dealing. Inside information includes the factors that determine the price of securities in the market.[16] Broadly speaking, inside information is defined as unpublished correct information that may substantially affect the price of securities and that relates to such securities or to the source of information.

The definition has four elements:

(i) First, the information must not have been previously published. This includes non-published information described as secret information, even if several people know this information, on condition they know that the information is confidential. It is not necessary that all people are familiar with the information for it to be published. It is enough if it becomes known by one or more persons who are interested in the information. Statistics and the analysis of the published data are not necessarily confidential information, even though they are unpublished.

(ii) Second, the information should be precise in that it is comprised of correct data rather than mere rumours. The disclosure of rumours does not constitute insider dealing.

(iii) The third element is that the information should be material, which requires that its publication will affect the price of the securities to which it relates.

---

15 Ahmed Almelhem, 'The Prohibition of Company Director from Buying or Selling the Shares of the Company during the Term of His Office' (2011) 35 *Journal of Law, University of Kuwait* 461.

16 Brenda Hannigan, *Insider Dealing* (2nd edn, Longman Group Ltd 1994) 2.

(iv) Finally, the information must relate to securities or to their issuing company. Such information can be internal in nature, such as information that discloses the occurrence of high profits and rewards, or it can be external information, which discloses that another company has agreed to a merger with the issuing company.[17]

### 7.2.2.3 How Is the Information Transferred?

A person could obtain inside information from an inside source directly, such as being a director or through a family relationship, or indirectly, for example, a family member to another person. In this respect, some laws require that to be charged with insider dealing, the person should have obtained the information from inside sources. Typically, if the person has not received the information from inside sources, they will not be convicted of any criminal offence or be subject to regulatory enforcement or attract any civil liability although this will depend on the jurisdiction.[18]

### 7.2.2.4 What Actions Are Banned?

There are two important points here: the first is the type of prohibited act, such as dealing with inside information, disclosing inside information, or encouraging other persons to trade. The second point is the scope of prohibition in terms of who is banned, namely, a company insider or an outsider who receives inside information.

### 7.2.3 Insider Dealing in the UK

Although insider trading in the UK has been illegal since 1980, it proved difficult to successfully prosecute individuals accused of it. There were several notorious cases where individuals were able to escape prosecution. Instead, the UK regulators relied on a series of fines to punish market abuses. These fines were widely perceived as an ineffective deterrent and there was a statement of intent by the UK regulator (the Financial Services Authority) to use its powers to enforce the legislation (specifically the Financial Services and Markets Act 2000). Between 2009 and 2012 the FSA secured 14 convictions in relation to insider dealing.

From a different viewpoint, insider dealing can be considered fraud because insider trades are based on an employer's information, especially

---

17  Ahmed Almelhem (n 208) 460.
18  Barry Rider, Kern Alexander, and Lisa Linklater (n 207) 6.

when the employer has trusted an employee to take care of it. In this situation, the insider misappropriates information belonging to the employer by breaching a fiduciary duty. However, the insider does not have a fiduciary duty to a trader. The misappropriation theory mentions that the insider breaches the confidential duty owed to the source of the data if they trade based on the employer's information. This will be discussed in detail later.

The UK Criminal Justice Act 1993 (CJA) section 57(1) defines an insider, section 57(2) defines an inside source, section 56[19] defines inside information, and section 52 defines prohibited activities.

In the UK, criminal lawsuits and civil sanctions for insider dealing offences are brought by the Financial Services Authority (now FCA). Few criminal prosecutions have been pursued because the standard of proof required to convict is higher than in civil actions. The criminal standard must show culpability beyond reasonable doubt, which is not easy with the type of evidence in such cases, because 'insiders' have many ways of concealing their tracks, including the use of nominees, offshore companies, and the like. Even if the evidence is uncovered, it must be corroborated, which is also difficult. The prosecution needs to establish that:

- An individual possessed inside information.
- They knew that such information was inside information.
- An individual traded in such inside information.
- The individual traded knowing that such information had come from an inside source.

In most cases, there will be no direct evidence that a person possessed inside information. In the case of *R v Holyoak, Hill and Morl* (unreported),[20] the prosecution failed to prove that when the defendants traded in the shares of a takeover target, the information that the defendants held was price-sensitive inside information. The defendants effectively disputed the charge by establishing that they thought that the information upon which they relied in their dealings had been publicly disclosed. On the other hand, in the case

---

19 In the United Kingdom, information can be defined as inside information if the following four conditions are met:

Relates to particular securities or to a particular issuer of securities or to particular issuers of securities and not to securities generally or to issuers of securities generally.

Is specific or precise.

Has not been made public.

If made public, it would likely have a significant effect on the price of any securities.

20 An account of the case is given by Jane Mayfield in an article entitled 'The FSA's Approach to Insider Dealing' (2009) 159 NLJ 7373.

of *R v (1) McQuoid (2) Melbourne*,[21] the prosecution was successful. The jury found that Melbourne had received inside information from McQuoid, in reliance upon which Melbourne made a profit. The court ordered the FSA (now FCA) to freeze the profit and sentenced each defendant to eight months in prison.

The 2008 financial crisis in the UK led the FSA (now FCA) to prosecute more criminal cases to deter insiders. The policy of 'credible deterrence' paid dividends with six successful prosecutions between 2009 and 2011.[22] Since then, there have been 27 convictions.[23] The FCA uses its power of investigation provided by the FSMA 2000 to achieve this success, present evidence, and prosecute insider dealing as defined in the CJA 1993.[24]

The UK has a dual criminal and civil regime for insider dealing.[25] Thus, the FCA has two options to follow. First, under the CJA it may prosecute an inside dealer through the courts. This can lead to prison. The second option is under the market abuse regime, which can lead to an unlimited fine. This is effected without going to court, through the FCA discipline committee.

The FSMA 2000 defines seven types of market abuse contained in the EU 2003 directive and is probably the most comprehensive definition of this activity. This is in addition to the definition of insider dealing in the 1993 Act.

The first three forms of market abuse are considered to be types of insider dealing.[26] These are defined in the 2000 Act as follows:

1) The first type of behaviour is where an insider deals, or attempts to deal, in a qualifying investment or related investment on the basis of inside information relating to the 'investment in question'. This type of abuse can be described as insider dealing.
2) The second is where an insider discloses inside information to another person otherwise than in the proper course of the exercise of his employment, profession, or duties. This type of abuse can be described as the wrongful disclosure of inside information.

21  (2009) Southwark Crown Court. After the buying process on 1 June, the price jumped to 45 pence per share after the takeover offer was announced. Melbourne earned approximately £48,900. Three months later, he gave half of the money that he had made from the deal to McQuoid.

22  Iain MacNeil (n 1) 414.

23  <www.fca.org.uk/news/three-charged-with-insider-dealing>.

24  Mayfield (n 213) 73.

25  Martyn Hopper, 'Overview of Market Conduct Regulation in the UK' in Martyn Hopper and others (eds), *A Practitioner's Guide to the Law and Regulation of Market Abuse* (Sweet & Maxwell 2013) 10–11.

26  Ibid 11.

3) The third is where the behaviour (not falling within subsection [2] or [3]) (a) is based on information, which is not generally available to those using the market, but which, if available to a regular user of the market, would be, or would be likely to be, regarded by them as relevant when deciding the terms on which transactions in qualifying investments should be effected, and (b) is likely to be regarded by a regular user of the market as a failure on the part of the person concerned to observe the standard of behaviour reasonably expected of a person in their position in relation to the market.

This type of abuse can be described as the wrongful use of inside information. As can be seen from the foregoing, market abuse is defined very broadly to cover market and off-market behaviour.[27] Market abuse can be committed by one person or more and according to the 2000 Act it is likely to be flexible.[28]

### 7.2.4 Insider Dealing in the US

The US Securities and Exchange Commission (SEC) defines illegal insider trading as:

> The buying or selling a security, in breach of a fiduciary duty or other relationship of trust and confidence, on the basis of material, non-public information about the security.

'Material information' is any information that could substantially impact an investor's decision to buy or sell the security. Non-public information is information that is not legally available to the public.

In the US, there is a complicated regulatory structure that regulates the securities industry.[29] The top regulatory agency is the Securities and Exchange Commission (SEC) which has to oversee all stock exchanges and all who trade in securities. In 2007, the Financial Industry Regulation Authority (FINRA) was created. This is a self-regulatory organisation which is responsible for policing the securities industry. It also sets rules for stockbrokers and licenses them, and can fine individuals and firms. The FINRA is responsible for customer complaints about any illegal or unethical actions.

---

27 Barry Rider and Kern Alexander, *Market Abuse and Insider Dealing* (2nd edn, Tottole 2009) 78.

28 Edward Swan and John Virgo, *Market Abuse Regulation* (2nd edn, OUP 2010) 215.

29 <http://stocks.about.com/od/tradingbasics/a/Regulat011705.htm>.

In terms of laws, individual states also have securities divisions.[30] They are different from state to state. It can be said that in the US there is a multi-fractioned regulatory system that includes federal and state bodies.

The Division of Enforcement was established in 1972 and acts as a police force. It is responsible for collecting evidence of possible securities law violations and recommending prosecution when needed. The SEC only handles civil matters that carry civil penalties, whereas the Justice Department concerns itself with criminal matters that carry imprisonment or similar penalties. Criminal cases fall under the jurisdiction of law enforcement agencies within the Department of Justice. However, the SEC often works closely with such agencies to provide evidence and assist with court proceedings.

Some of the most common securities law violations are manipulation of market prices, stealing a customer's fund or securities, insider trading, violating the broker-dealers' responsibility to treat customers fairly, and mis-representation or omission of material facts relating to securities. Evidence is gathered through market surveillance activities, investor complaints, other divisions of the SEC, and other securities industry sources.

Thus, the definition of an insider in the US has changed and has been extended to include:[31]

i. *Insiders*: this term covers all corporate employees.
ii. *Constructive insiders*: in some situations, information is revealed legit-imately to a professional person, such as an accountant or a lawyer working for the company, but not employed by the company. Such an outsider may become a fiduciary of shareholders because the outsider entered a special confidential relationship with the company, and the information is disclosed to them in confidence. However, this idea of treating an outsider as an insider based on their relationship, in which there is an expectation of confidentiality, was not universally accepted. In *Dirks*, for example, the Court stated that an individual must expressly or implicitly enter a fiduciary relationship with the issuer.
iii. *Tippers and tippees*: tippees can be held liable provided two conditions are met. The tipper must have breached a fiduciary duty to the company by making the tip, and the tippee must know or have reason to know of the breach.
iv. *Non-traditional relationship*: beyond the above traditional relation-ships, matters become complicated, and each case must be exam-ined on its merits. For example, is a doctor who learned confidential

---

30  Ibid.
31  Stephen Bainbridge, *An Overview* (n 202) 14–20.

information from a patient an insider? Similarly, is there a fiduciary relationship between spouses?

v. *Legislators*: another category of non-traditional insider is that of a legislator, like a member of Congress, who can access material non-public information in a variety of ways, such as in a Congressional hearing.

There is a time frame for the use of inside information, which is the period before the information reaches the public.[32] Many scholars maintain that the ban against dealing should not end just when the inside information is made public: an insider must wait for public investors to have an opportunity to act on it.[33]

In the US, two types of non-public information are specified. One is information that derives from internal corporate sources and is classed as 'inside information'. The other is 'market information' that originates outside of the company and affects the price of its securities but does not relate to its assets or earning power. The use of either is prohibited. Three sources of US law have contributed to the development of the insider trading regime: the 1934 Act (statute), the courts (common law), and the rules promulgated by the SEC. Each of the three sources has affected the insider trading regime over time, starting in 1934 and most recently in 2000.[34]

One overriding difference between the US regime on insider trading and that of the UK regime is in the promulgation and application of the law. In the US, the Securities Exchange Act 1934 does not mention insider dealing let alone define it. Reference is made to 'use or employ...any manipulative or deceptive device or contrivance'. It is left to the judges to decide according to common law whether an act constitutes insider dealing. On the other hand, the UK statute makes specific reference to insider dealing and prohibits it.

### 7.2.5 Insider Dealing in Kuwait

Kuwaiti law[35] seems to be less effective in the campaign against insider dealing. No framework of exact laws regulating insider dealing exists in

---

32 Saleh Alberbari, 'Stock Marts and Use of the Inside Information by Insiders: A Comparative Legal Study'. (Paper presented to the Conference of Securities Markets and Stock Exchanges, United Arab Emirates University College of Sharia and Law) 26.

33 Stephen Bainbridge, *An Overview* (n 202) 12.

34 <www.sechistorical.org/museum/galleries/it/takeCommand_d.php>.

35 As mentioned in Chapter 1, Islamic law is one source of Kuwaiti law. Accordingly, it would be wise to know the attitude of Islamic law toward insider dealing. From the viewpoint of Islam, insider dealing is fraud, termed '*taghrir*'. In general, any kind of fraud in any matter between individuals is illegal in Islam. Fraud is defined as a heinous and serious moral

Kuwait, although the Kuwait Capital Markets Act 2010 was passed to regulate the administration of the Stock Exchange and the trading of securities. The main advantage of the 2010 Act is that it provides criminal protection through provisions set out in Chapter 11, which make insider dealing a crime.

Before the 2010 Act, it could be clearly seen from the Kuwaiti Law of Commercial Companies Article No 140 that members of the board of directors were banned from buying or selling shares of the company upon whose board they served. Some commentators describe this as a unique action in comparison with other laws.[36]

Article 195 of the Companies Act 2016 states that:

> The chairman or a member of the board of directors, even if he is representing a natural or legal person, may not exploit any information received by him in his position to gain any benefit for himself or for any third party. Furthermore, he may not dispose, in any way whatsoever, over any shares of the company in which he is a member of the board of directors during his tenure unless he receives the approval of the Authority. The Authority shall issue the rules regulating the trading of shares in the company and manner of disclosure.

Article 164 of the new Act provides:

> This law is a special law, its provisions are also special provisions, and this law shall repeal all laws in public or private law that are contrary to its provisions.

Consequently, the Act regulates the nature of the work of a member of the board of directors, because each such member is an insider according to Article 118. Based on the authority of Articles 164s and 118 of the 2010 Act, Article 140 of the Kuwaiti Law of Commercial Company was repealed.

It should be noted that although insider dealing has been criminalised in Kuwait it still does not have a clear definition. As a result, there is much

---

wrong. *Taghrir* involves using actions or words to mislead another. *Taghrir* might also occur in certain conditions and agreements well-known as a 'trust sale'. So, the seller has the complete duty to disclose to the buyer all facts that could affect the price and the buyer's decision to buy. In this respect, the definition of *taghrir* under the law of Islam is similar to the position of the American SEC Rule 10b-5. Abdul Jabbar Siti, 'Insider Dealing: Fraud in Islam?' (2012) *Journal of Financial Crime*.

36  Ahmed Almehem (n 227) 437.

room for improvement. Combating insider dealing would be more effective if a new law were passed or if market rules were issued.

The Kuwaiti legislature has not clearly defined the offence of insider dealing. Some researchers define the offence as an action by an insider, who personally benefits from inside information or who benefits others before the information becomes public in breach of the rules of justice, transparency, and equality between dealers and outsiders.[37]

The Kuwaiti legislature provides in Article 1 of the Kuwait Capital Markets Act 2010 that:

> An insider is any person who, due to his position, is informed of fundamental information or data regarding a listed company, which was not available to the public.

This definition presents four conditions that must be met for a person to be classed as an insider.

(i)   *Due to his position*: the Kuwaiti legislation does not define 'position' in terms of the person's relationship with the employer or with the shareholders with whom they deal. As a result, the extent to which a tippee, an outsider, or a third party is included within this definition is uncertain.

(ii)  *Fundamental information or data*: while fundamental information or data consists of material information, this definition does not set out the boundaries of such information or data, nor does it identify the standard by which information or data are determined to be material.

(iii) *Listed company*: the same Article of the 2010 Act defines the listed company as any shareholding company listed on the stock exchange market.

(iv)  *Non-public information*: while it is important to describe a person as an insider when the information is not public knowledge, how can one determine whether information is public or not when the law does not provide a test to do this?

According to Article 118 of the 2010 Act, Kuwaiti law only bans the insider from doing one of the following actions:[38]

---

37 Adel Almane, 'Criminalization of Insider Dealing in Capital Market: Comparative Study between Kuwaiti and French Laws' (2012) *Journal of Law*, University of Kuwait 19.
38 Article 118 of the 2010 Act provides:
    Punishable by imprisonment for a term not exceeding five years and a fine not less than the value of the benefit achieved or losses that were avoided or the amount of ten thousand Dinars, whichever is higher, shall not exceed three times the value of the benefit achieved or losses that were avoided or the amount of one hundred thousand Dinars, whichever is

1) Benefitting from inside information. The legislature assumes that an insider can benefit from inside information if they know the nature of the information when buying or selling securities. The insider can refute this simple presumption through proof that they did not trade based on this information in Kuwait.[39]
2) Taking advantage of inside information.
3) Disclosing the inside information.
4) Giving advice based on inside information. Kuwaiti law limits the application of this article to the insider, which leaves unanswered the question of the outsider, especially the tippee.

In 2015, the law was amended to expand the definition of an insider to include a person 'who sold or purchased a security while in possession of Insider Information' and a person who 'disclosed Insider Information or gave an advice based on Insider Information to another Person'. This includes the person who receives and acts on such insider information. The law added a penalty of possible imprisonment for insider dealing. Furthermore, the Article stated that a fine could be imposed to the value of 'the amount of the benefit achieved, or losses avoided' or 'an amount of one hundred thousand Dinars – whichever is the higher'. Thus, the term insider was expanded as was the punishment for trading using insider information.

---

higher, or either penalties, any insider benefited or took advantage of inside information by buying or selling Securities or disclosure of inside information or to give advice on the basis of inside information to someone who will not be an insider. The person who is trading in Securities during the possession of internal beneficial information is described as an insider if the person is aware of them when buying or selling only if he could prove he did not trade on the basis of that information.

39 Ahmed Almelhem (n 208) 462.

# 8    Sanctions

Maintaining the integrity of financial markets is central to financial stability and growth in various countries. As discussed in Chapters 4 and 5, regulatory authorities have been established in different countries with a mandate to regulate the financial industry, make rules about financial trading, and enforce these laws in conjunction with the countries' law enforcement agencies.

This chapter focuses on the various types of sanctions that can be imposed by regulatory authorities and law enforcement agencies, as well as considering some of the specific instances of sanctions being imposed. This enables consideration of the questions: which are the most effective sanctions, and what approach should governments adopt?

There are three main types of sanctions:

1. Administrative or civil sanctions, imposed by a regulatory body.
2. Civil liability as imposed by courts of law.
3. Criminal sanctions.

## 8.1  Different Types of Sanctions

The two most important types of sanctions related to securities crimes are administrative (civil) and criminal sanctions. There are several administrative sanctions such as a temporary suspension from trading and fines. Criminal sanctions include prison sentences and criminal fines.

It should be noted that there is no civil sanction or provision allowing victims of securities crimes to sue inside dealers for damages to compensate them for any losses which they sustained because of the inside dealer's actions. One argument against having such provision is that it is difficult to prove that someone has been the victim of securities crimes. Neither the UK nor Kuwait allows for specific civil liability arising from securities crimes. The Kuwaiti legislature does impose criminal sanctions for insider dealing,

DOI: 10.4324/9781003301875-9

but it does not provide for specific civil liability. Consequently, the general rules of civil liability must be relied upon.

Some say that administrative (civil) sanctions for securities crimes should always be a financial penalty. A person convicted of securities crimes must return the profit made or the loss avoided. Some say that the funds should not go to the market players but should go to the state.[1] In just one year (2014) the FCA handed out a record of £1,471,431,800 in fines.[2]

## 8.2  Criminal or Civil Enforcement

Martin Wheatley, the former FCA chief executive, stated that fighting financial crime is not simple or straightforward. The enforcement mechanism needs a new style of regulation, new powers, and a new philosophy, with a clear mandate to pursue prosecution, impose unlimited fines, ban individuals from financial services and prevent, reduce, and deter future securities crimes. That cannot be achieved without having a sound regulatory authority.

Although some scholars completely disagree with the criminal provision in securities crimes, keeping the criminal sanction as an option is an excellent idea. It is argued that a criminal sanction is a major deterrent to securities crimes because there is the possibility of imprisonment. There is also the potential for the stigma of having been convicted of a crime that will follow the person throughout their life.[3]

Applying administrative (civil) sanctions is easier than applying criminal sanctions. For example, in the UK, until 2009, the FSA (now FCA) was reluctant to prosecute cases under criminal law because of the higher standard of proof required. However, with the arrival of the financial crisis, it has increased the number of criminal prosecutions, with a considerable rate of success, having secured 27 convictions related to insider dealing to date.[4] Therefore, some people feel criminal prosecution is a bigger deterrent than a civil action.

The most difficult problem with proving securities crimes is obtaining evidence, which can hinder the prosecution of those involved in this crime. One effective method of overcoming this problem is to give 'bounty rewards' to those who provide evidence that leads to a conviction. This practice exists in the US. For example, a bounty may be offered in the

---

1  R C H Alexander, *Insider Dealing and Money Laundering in the EU: Law and Regulation* (Ashgate 2007) 235.
2  <www.fca.org.uk/firms/being-regulated/enforcement/fines/2014>.
3  Ibid 232.
4  <www.fca.org.uk/news/three-charged-with-insider-dealing>.

amount of ten per cent of the civil penalty collected, if a person provides information that leads to civil penalties. Such a bounty encourages informants[5] and eases the difficulties involved in collecting evidence.[6]

Even though securities crimes have been criminalised in Kuwait, the need for comprehensive and effective laws is still not taken seriously in all developing countries, including Kuwait.

In Kuwait, a special court was established for civil and commercial matters relating to securities. Article 108 part 2 of the 2010 Law states that:

> 2 – Non-penal circuits with exclusive jurisdiction to decide on non-penal cases related to commercial, civil and administrative disputes arising from the implementation of the provisions of this Law and the regulations and bylaws related to the securities markets, and the disputes related to the enforcement of judgments issued thereby, regardless of the value of such disputes.

Since laws must provide a securities regime to punish those who breach the information disclosure regime, the civil liability, the criminal liability, and the administrative sanctions available must be considered.

## 8.3 Administrative (Civil) Penalties or Fines

In the UK, the FCA can impose administrative sanctions in the form of a fine, a public censure. Under s118 of the Financial Services and Markets Act 2000 (FSMA), the FCA can impose civil sanctions if the disclosure takes the form of market abuse. This regime also deals with misleading statements and practices. Section 118(c) defines inside information. Unless the rules permit delay, an RIS must be notified by issuers about inside information as soon as possible if the information concerning the issuer[7] is of a precise nature[8] and has significant effect;[9] this differs from issuer to issuer

---

5  Alan Palmiter, *Securities Regulation* (6th edn, Aspen Publishers 2014) 370.

6  Insider Trading and Securities Fraud Enforcement Act 1988 section 21A e (ITSFEA).

7  Michael Blair QC, George Walker, and Stuart Willey (n 170) 197.

8  s118 (d) states, 'information is precise if it (i) indicates circumstances that exist or may reasonably be expected to come into existence or an event that has occurred or may reasonably be expected to occur, and (ii) is specific enough to enable confusion to be drawn as to the possible effect of those circumstances or that event on the price of qualifying investment or related investments'.

9  According to s118 (d), 'information would be likely to have a significant effect on price if it is information of the kind which a reasonable investor would be likely to use as part of the basis of his investment decisions'.

depending on different factors, such as recent developments and the issuer's size.

In the UK, the FSA (now FCA) adopted a new policy in 2010[10] regarding the enforcement of financial penalties, as the result of which the number and amounts of fines increased. This was evidenced by the enormous size of the enforcement decision in 2013 against the Prudential Group which was fined £30 million for breaching FSA principles and UKLA listing principles.[11] The new policy is based on income. The penalty is up to 20 per cent of a firm's revenue from its business area and products. The penalty imposed on individuals who breach regulations in non-market abuse cases is up to 40 per cent of the individual's benefits and salary. The penalty in cases involving serious market abuse by an individual is a minimum of £100,000.[12] This policy seeks to achieve three objectives: disgorgement, deterrence, and discipline.[13] Its purpose is to change the behaviour of the market, as pointed out by Margaret Cole, FSA (now FCA) Director of Enforcement and Financial Crime, who stated that 'we believe enforcement penalties are a powerful tool to help change behaviour in the industry'.[14]

In Kuwait, administrative and disciplinary penalties are issued by a council called the Disciplinary Board. Article 140 of the 2010 Law mentions that:

> One or more disciplinary boards shall be established within the Authority, composed of three members headed by a judge delegated by the Supreme Judiciary Council and two members who are experienced in financial, economic, and legal affairs. The term of membership of the Disciplinary Board is three years and may be renewed.

The Board deals with the following matters:

(i) Deciding on the disciplinary matters referred to it by the Authority and concerning the violation of the provisions of this law, bylaws or any decisions or instructions issued in connection therewith.
(ii) Deciding on the appeals filed against the Securities Exchange decisions and the decisions taken by the Violations Committee thereat.

---

10  <www.fsa.gov.uk/pages/Library/Policy/Policy/2010/10_04.shtml>.
11  FSA/PH/031/2013; an enforcement decision was made by the FSA against Prudential Group PLC.
12  <www.fsac.org.uk/library/communication/pr/2010/036.html>.
13  Ibid.
14  Ibid.

The Disciplinary Board, when hearing these appeals, shall be deemed to act as an appellate body and its rulings with regard thereto shall be final. The Executive Bylaws shall set forth the system, rules, and procedures of the work of the Disciplinary Board and the manner in which it issues resolutions and notify the concerned parties thereof.

In Kuwait, the KCMA can apply one of the administrative penalties included in Law No 7 of 2010 if the issuer does not comply with the securities laws.

In terms of the 2015 Law, Article 146 authorises the KCMA to administer the following penalties:

1. Cautioning the violator to cease the violation.
2. Issuing a warning.
3. Requiring the violator to re-pass pre-qualification tests.
4. Suspending the violator's activities for a period not exceeding one year.
5. Suspension from practicing work or profession in final.
6. Suspending the license for a period not exceeding six months.
7. Revocation of the license.
8. Imposing restrictions on the activity or activities of the violator; such restrictions shall be specified by the Bylaws.
9. Cancelling the voting or proxy or power obtained by the violation of the provisions of this Law.
10. Suspending or cancelling any acquisition offer or purchase transactions outside the scope of the acquisition offer if they are in violation of the provisions of Chapter 7 of this Law or the Bylaws.
11. Prohibition of exercising voting rights for a period not more than three years by any person who refrained from submitting any statement, or submitted an incomplete statement, or one contrary to the truth or in violation with the Law or the Bylaws.
12. Suspending the validity of an applicable prospectus according to the provisions of this Law.
13. Cessation of trading of a security temporarily or suspension or cancellation of the decision to list a security before the effective date thereof.
14. Dismissal of a member of a board of directors or of a manager of one of the licensed companies or listed companies or investment controller or custodian of a collective investment scheme who failed to perform their duties as provided in this Law or the Bylaws.
15. Imposing financial penalties that are defined according to the severity of the violation not exceeding fifty thousand KD. In all cases, the Disciplinary Board may cancel all transactions related to the violation and the entailed effects or require the violator to pay amounts equal to the benefit they acquired or the value of the loss they have avoided as

a result of the violation. The amount may be multiplied if the person repeats the violations.

## 8.4  Soft Sanctions

In Kuwait, laws are sometimes divided into so-called 'hard law' and 'soft law'. Hard law refers to laws that are binding, authoritative, and effective, with penalties for breaches. However, a regulatory authority can also use so-called soft law,[15] which is the name given to statements of principles, codes of conduct, codes of practice, and guidance.[16] It is possible to mix hard and soft law, as in the corporate governance code in the UK. Although complying with the code is voluntary, listed companies are required to explain every instance of non-compliance.[17] This is referred to as the 'comply or explain' regime.

A comply or explain regime can be described as an alternative way to achieve strong regulation. It strikes a balance between soft law and hard law that can be suitable in today's complex economic world. The comply or explain approach has both advantages and disadvantages. Michelle Edkins, a corporate governance expert and Managing Director of Corporate Governance and Responsible Investment at BlackRock Inc., summarised the advantages and disadvantages of this system by saying that:

> 'Comply or explain' has its limitations, poor explanations, differences of opinion between management and shareholders, different views as to the right approach amongst shareholders, lack of resources for engagement, and limits on the scope of some shareholders to be pragmatic. Nonetheless, comply or explain offers more flexibility than the alternative. Companies can set out their case and, whether agreement is reached or not, engagement helps build mutual understanding. Communication about the future involves indicating plans to adopt and improve, which, for shareholders – the institutions and the private savers among our clients – provides reassurance that companies are being run for the long-term and in the interests of the shareholders.[18]

---

15 Although there are no financial penalties for breaching soft law, it can play a significant role in achieving a regulatory authority's objectives.

16 William Twining and David Miers, *How to Do Things with Rules* (5th edn, Cambridge University Press 2011) 43.

17 If the companies do not comply, they will breach the listing rules.

18 Michelle Edkins, 'Comply or Explain, An Essay on the Report Titled: Comply Or Explain: 20th Anniversary of the UK Corporate Governance Code' (London Stock Exchange, The Financial Reporting Council Limited 2012) 18.

Comply or explain means more flexibility in the application of the set of rules with no free passes for avoiding these rules. Companies are required to provide an explanation, and others, such as future investors and institutional investors, will judge and monitor. Although there is no action from a regulatory authority if the explanation is insufficient, the market forces the shareholders to act. The share price will force the shareholder to engage. Investing is about taking risks. An investor who buys stock in a company with high standards of corporate governance is less likely to lose money. Investment advisers will also take the statement of a code into account when giving advice.

The market, in general, and the shareholders, specifically, force the companies to follow the code.[19] Simply, the process for shareholders is that if no one wants to buy the company's shares, then the price will decrease, which prompts the shareholders to try to correct the situation. Consequently, the decline in the share price encourages the firm to adopt good corporate principles. The process is similar to the idea of market power on competitive policy that drives firms to improve their prices and services.[20] Shareholders will consider this noncompliance when deciding to buy, vote, hold, and sell their shares.[21]

The comply or explain code is constantly evolving. The former Chairman of the Financial Reporting Council, Baroness Sarah Hogg, acknowledged that although the UK Code benefits the market, such as making a difference in the corporate culture, there is still work that needs to be done to develop the Code further.[22] Andrew Keay criticised the comply or explain regime because no regulatory body assesses the companies' statements and there is no way to measure the extent to which these principles actually work, such as statistics. Shareholders do not really engage in monitoring their companies.[23] He suggested introducing regulatory oversight to examine whether each company complies and whether the explanations are adequate.[24]

19 Andrew Keay, 'Comply Or Explain: In Need of Greater Regulatory Oversight' (2012) SSRN Working paper <http://papers.ssrn.com/sol3/papers.cfm?abstract_id=2144132>.
20 Massimo Motta, *Competition Policy: Theory and Practice* (Cambridge University Press 2009) 41.
21 David Seidl, Paul Sanderson, and John Robert 'Applying "Comply Or Explain": Conformance with Codes of Corporate Governance in UK and Germany' (2009) University of Cambridge working paper.
22 Essay 'Comply Or Explain: 20th Anniversary of the UK Corporate Governance Code' (2012) London Stock Exchange, The Financial Reporting Council Limited 4–5.
23 Andrew Keay (n 251).
24 Ibid.

This gives rise to four considerations. One response to Keay's comment is that the content of the explanation is not important. For example, in Germany, the corporate governance code works under the 'comply or disclose' approach, under which the firms comply with the recommendations or disclose their noncompliance.[25] In this approach, firms comply or just say they will not comply.

Second, some provisions of the code are already in rules or law and are mandatory. The comply or explain regime is part of a large regulatory system. The code can be used as clear evidence of not complying with other rules and laws. The third point is that there is already a mechanism for judging the adequacy of an explanation under the Stewardship Code, under which institutional investors must act if they deem that an explanation is inadequate, and they must comply or explain any failure to take action. The Stewardship Code aims to help institutional investors (on behalf of clients and beneficiaries) to exercise their responsibilities properly under the comply or explain regime. Therefore, institutional investors will monitor their investee companies under a comply or explain regime by, for example, giving a timely written explanation if, after careful consideration, they do not accept the company's position.[26] The fourth point concerns enforcement of compliance by a regulatory authority. More rules will affect market competition.

There is no stewardship code in Kuwait. It would be better if there were a code under a 'comply or explain' system in these countries, which would rely on family companies to act.

## 8.5  Sanctions in the UK

The FCA has a range of powers to investigate and sanction individuals or companies who have breached the FSMA or the FCA's rules. It has the power to impose administrative sanctions on any person in respect of a breach of requirements. In instances where the regulator finds a breach of the rules has occurred, it has the power to impose sanctions directly. In these cases, it issues a decision notice, notifying the firm or individual of its findings and imposing what it considers to be the appropriate penalty. It will then be for the individual or firm to decide whether it wishes to refer the FCA's decision to a specialist court known as the Upper Tribunal, which

---

25  David Seidl, Paul Sanderson, and John Robert (n 253).

26  According to Principle 3 of the UK Stewardship Code 2012; 'Institutional Investors Should Monitor Their Investee Companies' <www.frc.org.uk/Our-Work/Publications/Corporate-Governance/UK-Stewardship-Code-September-2012.pdf>.

will hear the matter afresh. At the hearing, the court may determine the appropriate action to be taken.

In the context of securities, the key areas that the FCA tends to focus on in its civil enforcement actions include failures in a firm's governance, systems or controls, breaches of the Market Abuse Requirements ensuring disclosure and transparency in relation to price-sensitive information, civil market abuse offences, failures to properly advise on investments (where there is a duty to do so) or to comply with conduct of business or financial promotion rules, and individual failings of a firm's senior managers.

The FCA also has the power to investigate and prosecute certain criminal market misconduct offences, including insider dealing, making a false or misleading statement intended to induce someone to invest in securities, and creating a false or misleading impression in relation to relevant markets or securities or in respect of benchmarks. The FCA shares the power to prosecute those offences with other prosecutors including the Secretary of State for Business, Energy and Industrial Strategy, the Director of the Serious Fraud Office (SFO), and the Crown Prosecution Service. These agencies have agreed on broad principles that guide the decision as to which agency should investigate a suspected offence and, where more than one agency is investigating, how they should cooperate to avoid unnecessary duplication and ensure procedural fairness.

It should be noted that in the UK, the FCA has an extensive range of disciplinary, criminal, and civil powers according to FSMA 2000. This means that it has two choices. It could use one or all of them, as in the case of insider dealing, where it can resort to criminal proceedings or use its administrative powers to apply sanctions.[27]

## 8.6 Sanctions in the US

The SEC has the authority to impose penalties on consumers and corporations alike. It may bring civil actions or administrative actions seeking civil penalties or the return of illegal profits. The SEC also works with federal law enforcement agencies to investigate potential crimes and bring charges that could result in lengthy prison sentences. However, the penalties the SEC imposes on criminals are a little different from the penalties given for other financial crimes like theft or robbery. The primary difference is that the SEC does not have the ability to imprison anyone. Instead, the SEC imposes monetary penalties, forces the disgorgement of ill-gotten gains, and has the authority to restrict an individual's ability to work in the

---

27 <www.fca.org.uk/static/documents/enforcement-information-guide.pdf>.

securities industry or serve as an officer or director of a public company. Hence, while the SEC cannot impose prison sentences, it has the authority to force fraudsters to pay fines, give up any gains received through their fraudulent and misleading activities, and ruin the careers of white-collar criminals.

The SEC obtains billions of dollars each year in monetary sanctions from wrongdoers who have violated the federal securities laws. As a part of the SEC's enforcement responsibilities, it issues orders and administers judgments ordering securities violators to, among other things:

- Disgorge, or pay back, ill-gotten gains (not exceeding a wrongdoer's net profits) in order to return the funds to harmed investors.
- Pay civil monetary penalties (see the calculation of civil monetary penalties).
- Pay interest (pre-judgment and potentially post-judgment).

## 8.7  Sanctions in Kuwait

Article 139 of the 2010 Law states that:

> A violation is any act which is not in accordance with the rules, regulations, decisions, or instructions issued by the Authority within the framework of this Law.

Article 146 of the Kuwaiti Act 2010 provides that the disciplinary board may impose any of 17 different kinds of penalties, including a caution or warning, but it does not include any financial penalty.

Article 131 of the Kuwaiti Act 2010 gives the defendant and the Authority the option to reach a financial settlement at any time during the criminal trial. The offer of a settlement can be initiated by either party. The settlement amount shall not exceed the maximum fine and shall not be less than the minimum criminal fine stipulated in Article 118 of the 2010 Act. Apart from the potential financial advantage of reaching a settlement, there are other advantages, such as avoiding imprisonment and salvaging one's reputation.

It is possible to have two different sanctions for the same action. The law allows for a criminal and administrative sanction for the same action. Article 138 of 2010 Act mentions that:

> The reporting and the initiation of investigation by the Public Prosecution and filing of the criminal case shall not prevent the right of the Authority from taking disciplinary action. The Disciplinary Board

may defer the taking of disciplinary action pending the rendering of a final ruling in the matter of the criminal case. In all events, the penal court judgment shall be binding to all.

The Kuwaiti Act 2010 should mention the legal entity that is liable because criminal responsibility for a non-natural person is not accepted under the general rules. As a result, the legislature did not draw a clear policy for dealing with this issue. Kuwaiti law needs a special organisation to address this issue, similar to that created by Law 35 of 2002 Regarding Combating Money Laundering Operations, which provides in Article 12:

> [W]ithout prejudice to the criminal liability of a natural person stated therein, the companies of those persons who are criminally questionable for the crimes…shall be punished with a fine not exceeding one million Dinars if the crime is committed in its interest.[28]

In Kuwait, for crimes relating to insider dealing, a fine of a minimum of 1,000 but not exceeding 100,000 KD, but no imprisonment, is imposed upon any person who has omitted, withheld, or prevented material information for which the law required disclosure to the Authority or Stock Exchange regarding dealing or advising about selling or buying securities.[29]

---

28  Adel Almane (n 230) 31.
29  Kuwaiti Law 2010 Article 120.

# 9 Corporate Governance

Securities law is a wide-ranging topic that relates to listed companies and the rules imposed on them. Corporate governance relates to the way these companies conduct their business and how the information presented by these companies to the public is used in the trading of their securities. As a result, corporate governance failures can have major consequences for those involved in the trading of securities.

This chapter aims to highlight the most important principles that, if followed, can result in the company being well-managed and result in greater value for those who trade in its securities.

## 9.1 Introduction – What Is Corporate Governance?

The term 'corporate governance' is a complex term as it relates to various matters such as law, economics, management, accounting, and other subjects, each with its own developments. Corporate governance issues also include culture, ownership, and legal arrangements.[1] Therefore, due to its multi-faceted nature, defining corporate governance is not straightforward.[2] However, under the regulation of corporate governance, laws, rules, and standards define the relationship between a company's management, on the one hand, and shareholders and stakeholders (such as bondholders, workers, suppliers, creditors, and consumers), on the other hand.

The UK Corporate Governance Code 2018 states:

> Corporate governance is the system by which companies are directed and controlled. Boards of directors are responsible for the governance of their companies. The shareholders' role in governance is to appoint

---

1 Christine Mallin, *Corporate Governance* (4th edn, Oxford University Press 2013) 15.
2 Andrew Keay, *The Enlightened Shareholder Value Principle and Corporate Governance* (Routledge 2013) 6.

DOI: 10.4324/9781003301875-10

the directors and the auditors and to satisfy themselves that an appropriate governance structure is in place.

This makes it clear that corporate governance deals with the relationship between the board and the shareholders in governing and controlling the company.

The Kuwaiti legislature has defined governance in vague terms, stating that corporate governance is based on a set of rules that represent the foundation on which good governance practices in companies are based. These rules include a set of principles and methodology with the requirements needed to achieve the goals of governance.

It is important to note that the concept of corporate governance is based on two points. One is about control of the day-to-day operations of the business and the other is about the future direction of the company. Since there are competing interests within a company, corporate governance provides the system of rules, practices, and processes by which the company is directed and controlled.

Corporate governance can be likened to controlling a car, which involves controlling the steering wheel, the brake, and the accelerator to ensure that the car reaches its destination.[3] This means that corporate governance rules have the potential to define the authority, the approach to risk management, and how to protect a company and its investors. Consequently, corporate governance is about the relationship between the boards and managers and between the boards and its investors by guiding company actions and monitoring their performance.[4]

### 9.1.1 *Aim of Corporate Governance*

The objectives of corporate governance codes vary from one country to another. According to the UK Code 2012, its goal is to deliver a company's long-term success by facilitating effective, entrepreneurial, and prudent management. Corporate governance is about good management by the board. The code is a guide to good management practices.

In the US, there is no official corporate governance code. Each state is entitled to enact its own set of laws and regulations, creating fiduciary and managerial responsibilities that bind a company's management, shareholders, and the board within a larger, societal context defined by legal, regulatory, competitive, economic, democratic, ethical, and other societal forces.

---

3  Donald Nordberg, *Corporate Governance Principles and Issues* (SAGE 2011) 7.
4  Ibid 5.

In Kuwait, the Code of 2015 places the issuing of corporate governance rules under the control of the Capital Markets Authority. It states the importance of establishing proper rules for corporate governance to achieve justice, competitiveness, and transparency in the market. Rules of governance here are about principles, systems, and procedures that better protect shareholders. In addition, they state that good governance is based on the promotion of three points. First, ethical behaviour to ensure commitment to ethics and good professional conduct; second, oversight and accountability and, finally, administrative organisation to ensure the proper distribution of powers and responsibilities and the separation of functions.

### 9.1.2  Corporate Governance Principles

Several possible corporate governance areas have developed over time. These include:

- Board composition (leadership).
- Board effectiveness.
- The role of board committees.
- Risk management
- Remuneration.
- Relationships with shareholders.
- Bribery and corruption.
- IT governance.
- Mergers and acquisition.
- Succession planning.
- Sustainability and climate change.
- Proxy access.

It is difficult to find fixed rules of governance that are suitable for every situation because governance rules for protecting the nation differ from governance rules for shareholders and creditors, etc.[5] Corporate governance needs to be developed over time. For example, in the UK, the Financial Reporting Council (FRC)[6] has stated that, even though the level of corporate

---

5 Donald Nordberg (n 264) 54.
6 The Financial Reporting Council (FRC) is an independent regulator in the UK. One of the FRC's missions is to promote high quality corporate governance by setting the code and monitoring its impact. In 2003, the FRC took responsibility for the UK corporate governance code. The FRC's board comprises of 14 members, some of them executive and some non-executive members. The board has three committees. <www.frc.org.uk/Home.aspx>.

governance standards is high, there still is room for improvement.[7] After the financial crisis of 2007/2008, the level of governance standards in Britain was shown to be higher than anywhere else in the world.[8] However, this did not prevent the crisis from happening.

In the last ten years, corporate governance legislation has appeared in several countries to increase investor protection and confidence, especially in stock markets.[9] Corporate governance principles do not remain static but evolve with the surrounding developments and must continue to develop. For example, the Organisation for Economic Co-operation and Development (OECD) issued the Principles of Corporate Governance in 1999. The OECD governments agreed to revise new principles in 2004.[10] Ensuring the basis for an effective corporate governance framework, ensuring the equitable treatment of shareholders (including minority and foreign shareholders), protecting the rights of shareholders, disclosure and transparency, the role of stakeholders in corporate governance, and the effective monitoring of and by the board (responsibilities of the board) are among the most important areas covered by corporate governance principles.[11]

In the UK 2012 Code, there are main principles, supporting principles, and provisions. There are five main principles (A–E) pertaining to leadership, effectiveness, accountability, remuneration, and relations with shareholders. Accordingly, the UK code is a guide to effective board practice.

### 9.1.3 The Effect on Investors of Failures of Corporate Governance

There are different types of failure of corporate governance, such as poor risk management, fraud, fictitious transactions, corruption, financial manipulation (such as LIBOR manipulation), rogue trading, and personal interest. The causes of these problems are always due to mismanagement.

It is thought that the reason for corporate scandals is the result of the hijacking of management theory from the main economic opinions in the 1980s, by focusing on increasing shareholder returns, such as large

---

7 Financial Reporting Council (FRC), 'Development in Corporate Governance 2011: The Impact and Implementation of the UK Corporate Governance and Stewardship Codes' (December 2011) 1.

8 Andrew Chambers, *Corporate Governance Handbook* (5th edn, Bloomsbury Professional 2012) 350.

9 Christine Mallin (n 262) 26.

10 Fianna Joesover and Grant Kirkpatrick, 'The Revised OECD Principles of Corporate Governance and Their Relevance to Non-OECD Countries' (2005) 3.

11 Ibid 7–9.

dividends, at the expense of retaining and reinvesting profits, including research and development, which caused false economic progress.[12] The failures were caused by management problems, not economic problems. As a result, corporate governance principles can be described as an intervention in the management of the company that aims to reduce the likelihood of such company failures.

Lynn Stout, a former Professor of Corporate and Business Law at the Cornell Law School, stated that the drive to maximise shareholder value by focusing on short-term earnings affects stakeholder goals, including long-term investors. It stops the growth of the company as there is a conflict between the rising shareholder value and the development of the company. She mentioned that the solution is to build good boards of directors instead of shareholder value thinking.[13] The idea of focusing only on shareholder value did not exist 50 years ago, because the company goals were not the same. The focus was not only on shareholders, but also on providing greater protection to employees and society in general.[14] There is no law which requires managers to increase the share price of a company. The drive to do this is purely the doing of managers themselves.[15]

## 9.2  Why Is Corporate Governance Important?

As early as the 1970s a few corporate scandals started to emerge which highlighted the risk to an investor's shareholding from the irresponsible, negligent, and even fraudulent or near fraudulent actions of those responsible for governing a company leading to a fall in company value and even its complete collapse.[16] This trend continued into the twenty-first century culminating in the 2008 financial crisis.[17] This section considers the measures taken to regulate failures in corporate governance.

Good corporate governance is needed to protect individual investors by preventing and reducing the occurrence of company scandals in the future and ensuring that the company protects the value on behalf of shareholders.

---

12 Simon Caulkin, 'Management Theory Was Hijacked in the 1980s' *The Guardian* (London, 28 June 2013) <www.guardian.co.uk/commentisfree/2012/nov/12/management-theory-hijacked>.

13 Lynn Stout, *The Shareholder Value Myth: How Putting Shareholders First Harms Investors, Corporations, and the Public* (Berrett Koehler Publishers 2012) 83–85.

14 Ibid 3.

15 Ibid 4.

16 Bob Ticker, *Corporate Governance: Principles, Polices and Practices* (3rd edn, Oxford University Press 2015) 11.

17 Ibid 15.

Corporate governance is multi-faceted, and other aspects of corporate governance affect listed companies, such as risk management, bribery, fraud, and poor board practice. In recent years, several scandals and collapses have not only reduced shareholders' financial investment, but have also affected other stakeholders, such as employees who have lost their jobs and, in many cases, their pension funds as well. Better enforcement methods of corporate governance compliance have the potential to reduce lapses of corporate governance and boost investor confidence, economic efficiency, and growth.

In companies in which ownership and management are separate, as in the case of listed companies, there is a danger that a director, by virtue of their powers, could put the company at risk or abuse their position.[18] This is a worldwide problem, as illustrated by the examples below.[19] Numerous scandals and collapses have occurred in different countries because of the shortcomings in the way that companies are operated. Therefore, no country is immune from such problems. Where gaps exist between owners and managers (separation of ownership and control),[20] corporate governance principles can be used as one method of improving the performance of listed companies and, therefore, better protect retail investors against the risk of poor corporate governance.

Good corporate governance does not only aim to protect investors, but it also has the potential to affect a company's overall success. Some say that there is a relationship between the success of the company and corporate governance.

---

18  Erik Vermeulen, 'Beneficial Ownership and Control: A Comparative Study – Disclosure, Information and Enforcement' (2013) OECD Corporate Governance Working Papers 7, 8 <www.oecd-ilibrary.org/governance/oecd-corporate-governance-working-papers_22230939>.

19

| Year | Country | Company |
|------|---------|---------|
| 2001 | US | Enron |
| 2003 | Italy | Parmalat, known as Europe's Enron |
| 2008 | UK | Royal Bank of Scotland (RBS) |
| 2009 | India | Satyam |
| 2012 | Japan | Olympus Corporation |

Christine Mallin (n 262) 2–7.

20  There are various theories about what corporate governance means, but the predominant theory is the 'agency theory', which considers the shareholders to be the principals and the directors to be their agents. Thus, there is a separation of ownership and control; ibid 16–18.

## 9.3 Corporate Governance Principles

This section considers different features of good corporate governance. Where possible, practical real-world examples are given to illustrate the points being highlighted.

### 9.3.1 Risk Management

Without doubt, proper risk management is likely to decrease the occurrence of company scandals and collapse.[21] There are four major risk groups, and each company must identify the four categories and the links between them, knowing what is acceptable and what the company can bear.

1) *Financial risks*: these include debt and interest rates, poor financial management, asset losses, and accounting problems. This type can be controlled by the company.
2) *Operational risks*: relate to poor capacity management, employee issues (fraud, bribery, and corruption), and cost overruns. This group can also be controlled by the company.
3) *Strategic risks*: these are external factors such as pricing pressure, partner losses, and industry downturns.
4) *Hazard risks*: hazards include political issues, natural disasters, terrorism, and legal issues.

The last two groups cannot be controlled by the company. This analysis shows that there are financial and non-financial risks.[22] The question here is how to protect investors from risk management by using corporate governance. Managers can misuse their position to achieve something at the expense of the company that is not in the company's interests, such as gaining personal benefits, misbehaviour by managers, or just increasing the company's profits.

Some say that the core of the problem is caused by separating ownership and control in managing other people's money,[23] which is the so-called agency theory. These problems may be avoided in the future by applying corporate governance principles. However, there is a danger that by intro-

---

21 Luca Enriques and Dirk Zetzsche, 'The Risky Business of Regulating Risky Management in Listed Companies' (2013) 10(3) *European Company and Financial Law Review* 1, 2.
22 Alpesh Shah, 'Corporate Governance for Main Market and AIM companies' (2012) White paper, London Stock Exchange 104.
23 Alessio Pacces, *Rethinking Corporate Governance: The Law and Economics of Control Powers* (Routledge 2012) 3.

ducing more regulations, economic growth will be affected. It is impossible to prevent such occurrences simply by passing laws and regulations. The quality of management must be improved to make it more ethical to stop managers engaging in and turning a blind eye to dishonest practices, with greater vigilance to stop others in the company from engaging in such practices.

### 9.3.2 Independent Directors

One way to avoid mismanagement by the board of directors is to include independent directors in its make-up. In general, a director or a member of a board of directors can be described as an independent director[24] if they do not have a material or financial relationship with the company or related persons. Having independent directors has several advantages. They assist the company to achieve a balance of power by increasing the quality of board oversight and reducing the possibility of damaging conflicts of interest.[25] This will likely affect the company's performance, which will reduce the chance of maladministration and maximise shareholder value.[26]

In the US, there has been a shift to add more independent directors to the board of directors in listed companies. Consequently, from 1950 to 2005, the percentage of independent directors increased from 20% to 75%.[27] In 2012, at least 75% of the members of the board of directors of 93 of the Top 100 American firms were independent directors.[28] This indicates a trend of increasing the number of independent directors in the NYSE.

The NYSE Listing Manual Rules require that a majority of the board members be independent.[29] When a company falls below the independence majority requirements, it has to disclose this fact to the NYSE while it seeks a new independent director. While no specific number of independent directors is stipulated, it must be a majority. As noted above, the modern trend is to have 75% of the board as independent.

Kuwait has approached the issue differently by requiring a minimum and maximum number of independent directors. In Kuwait, the Kuwait Corporate Governance Code (KCGC) mentions that any listed companies

---

24 Known as an outside director.
25 Section 303A.01 Corporate Governance Standards, NYSE.
26 Corporate governance principles are at the same time important and dangerous because they possess the potential to develop a company or to reduce its performance.
27 Jeffrey N Gordon, 'The Rise of Independent Directors in the United States, 1950–2005: Of Shareholder Value and Stock Market Prices' (2006/7) 59 *Stan L Rev* 1465.
28 <https://content.next.westlaw.com/Document/I>.
29 Section 303A Corporate Governance Standards, NYSE.

should have a minimum of one independent director, while the maximum number should not exceed half the number of members of the board of directors.[30] The Kuwaiti legislator took the 'minimum and the maximum standard' approach and did not leave the company the option to determine the number of independent directors on its own. Nevertheless, the majority standard requires that the listed company board consist of a majority of non-executive members.

The process of determining the independence of a director is extremely important to the concept of independent directors. The most important part of the independence test relates to who is responsible for determining whether a director is independent.

According to NYSE rules, one of the board's responsibilities is to determine who is independent, and who is not. The actual NYSE standards state that

> No director qualifies as 'independent' unless the board of directors affirmatively determines that the director has 'no material relationship' with the listed company, either directly or as a partner, shareholder or officer of an organization that has a relationship with the company.

Therefore, NYSE boards are left to their own devices to determine who is independent. The test for independence comes down to the three words: no material relationship.

In Kuwait, according to KSE rules, the board has no responsibility to determine the independence of a director. This makes the determination process more complex.

### 9.3.3 *Internal Audit Systems*

Another important control mechanism is the internal audit system. The concept of internal auditing is not new and has a long history with a variety of different applications such as bookkeeping.[31] It has evolved remarkably

---

30  Article 2-2 of Rule I, 'Construct a Balanced Board Composition' of the Executive Bylaws related to Corporate Governance 2015 states, 'The following must be complied with Board composition: [...] 3 – Majority of members of a board of directors must be non-executive members. It shall include one independent member at least. However, independent members shall not exceed half the members of a board of directors'.

31  Institute of Internal Auditors Association Research Foundation, *Internal Audit Capability Model*, <https://na.theiia.org/iiarf/>.

over the last 60 years.[32] However, in recent times the role of internal audit-ing has become more important than ever before. This is due to the increase in corporate scandals and financial mismanagement by boards of directors and unscrupulous management of companies.

First, the scope of internal auditing has rapidly extended and listed com-panies have been forced to implement internal auditing systems, such as those in the Kuwait Stock Exchange and the NYSE. Second, the internal auditing function has expanded to cover management control and account-ing, assisting external auditors, and other related functions. As a result, the current definition of an internal audit system can be described as, 'An inter-nal audit system is an independent and objective assurance and advisory activity that aims to increase value and enhance the organization's func-tions'.[33] The scope of its role covers four important areas:

1. Enhancement of organisational value.
2. Protection of organisational value by providing risk-based and objec-tive assurances by limiting the risk of fraud.[34]
3. Advice.
4. Insight.

The Committee of Sponsoring Organizations (COSO)[35] published a frame-work in which it defined an internal control as a 'process, effected by an entity's board of directors, management and other personnel, designed to provide reasonable assurance regarding the achievement of objectives relat-ing to operations, reporting and compliance'.[36] The COSO was established in 1985 in the US. Its main aims were to assist companies and organisations with financial controls and reporting systems as well as in assessing their control systems. This framework was named as an example of a 'suitable control framework' by the Securities and Exchange Commission (SEC) and has been used by listed companies ever since. The framework was updated in 2013.

---

32 Ibid.
33 Institute of Internal Auditors Association Research Foundation, *Guidance Notes* <https:// na.theiia.org/standards-guidance/mandatory-guidance/Pages/Definition-of-Internal -Auditing.aspx>.
34 Hans-Ulrich Westhausen, 'The Escalating Relevance of Internal Auditing as Anti-Fraud Control' (2017) 2 *J Financial Crime* 223.
35 The Committee of Sponsoring Organizations (COSO) of the National Commission on Fraudulent Financial Reporting, also known as the Treadway Commission.
36 Committee of Sponsoring Organizations, Home Page <www.coso.org/Pages/default.asp>.

The COSO framework includes the following objectives:

1. Objectives pertaining to the company's operations (including operational and financial) with a view to improving the effectiveness and efficiency.
2. Those relating to the internal and external reporting of the company, focusing particularly on such matters as reliability, transparency, and other items required by regulators.
3. Objectives relating to compliance with laws, rules, and regulations specific to each organisation.

The COSO framework states that internal control consists of five interrelated components as follows:

1) *Control environment*: this includes the standards, processes, and structures that are applied throughout the business. The board of directors and management are tasked with setting these standards and enforcing them (as well as applying them).
2) *Risk assessment*: this involves the process of identifying and analysing the risks to the business, as well as planning how to deal with these. The board will consider a wide range of factors that could affect the business and how to deal with these effectively.
3) *Control activities*: these comprise actions carried out as a result of the policies and procedures established by management with a view to lowering the risks associated with the business objectives. They are performed throughout the business in all departments and in all stages of doing business.
4) *Information and communication*: these are vital for any business to be successful. Accurate information is particularly important in the internal control systems and responsibilities. Communication occurs within the company and between various departments. This allows the business to carry out its objectives, as well as provides personnel with the relevant information relating to internal control responsibilities and their importance.
5) *Monitoring activities*: the internal auditor is required to constantly evaluate the various components of the internal control systems with a view to ensuring that the abovementioned principles are present and functioning. In the event of any errors being detected or if any improvements can be made, the internal auditor should communicate with the senior management about this.

According to the Institute of Internal Auditors (IIA)[37] based in North America,[38] the core principles of having an effective internal audit are that it should:

1) Prove integrity.
2) Prove competence and due professional care.
3) Be independent.
4) Be in line with the strategies, objectives, and risks of the organisation.
5) Be appropriately positioned and adequately resourced.
6) Prove quality and continuous improvement.
7) Communicate effectively with others.
8) Provide risk-based assurance.
9) Be insightful, proactive, and future-focused.
10) Help organisational improvement.[39]

The IIA Standards are an accepted best practice of the internal audit function in several stock exchanges, such as the NYSE.[40]

Countries around the world have different approaches to the requirements of internal auditing. For example, the concept of 'freedom to choose' is applied in countries in the EU that do not require compulsory internal audit functions in their corporate governance codes.[41] In contrast, some countries, such as the UK, require companies to have internal audit systems, but do not enforce this requirement. This has led to the development of the 'comply or explain' principle that allows companies to comply or explain in their financial reports why they choose not to have internal audit systems. Furthermore, some stock exchanges make it a compulsory requirement to

---

37  The Institute of Internal Auditors (IIA) establishes standards for the internal audit profession and provides certifications in internal auditing.
38  The IIA was established in 1941. It is an international professional association and a recognised authority, acknowledged leader, chief advocate, and principal means of professional education. It has more than 185,000 members.
39  The Institute of Internal Auditors, *Core Guidance* <https://na.theiia.org/standards-guidance/mandatory-guidance/Pages/Core-Principles-for-the-Professional-Practice-of-Internal-Auditing.aspx>.
40  Around 400 of the largest securities firms in America are members of the New York Stock Exchange. The NYSE rules play an important role in monitoring and regulating the activities of its members, member firms and listed companies, as well as enforcing compliance with NYSE rules and federal securities laws.
41  Ismael and Roberts (n 26), 'Factors Affecting the Voluntary Use of Internal Audit: Evidence from the UK' (2018) 33(3) *Managerial Auditing Journal* 290.

have an internal control function (IAF). These include the NYSE and the KSE. Hence, there is no clear standard about auditing culture around the world, and there is a lack of clear guidance from regulators about what they require.[42] This has created confusion for companies and has led to some companies avoiding compliance or not strictly applying good corporate governance principles.

### 9.3.4  Formation of Committees

One of the most important supporting principles under corporate governance codes is to form committees.

Kuwait requires the formation of five committees. According to the Kuwaiti Corporate Governance Code 2013, each board must form five different types of committee:

1) *Audit committee*: according to principle 4/2, the board of directors must form a committee concerned with internal audit. Its primary role is to ensure the integrity of the financial reporting and internal control systems and to recommend the nomination of the external auditor to the board. Thereafter, the general assembly appoints the external auditor in accordance with the nomination of the board of directors.
2) *Risk management committee*: the company must form a committee concerned with risk management according to principle 5/2.
3) *Governance committee*: the board of directors must form a committee concerned with the application of governance according to principle 5/4.
4) *Nomination committee*: according to principle 3/1, the board of directors must form a committee concerned with nominations for appointment. Its primary role is to prepare recommendations on all proposed nominations to achieve the perfect selection of competent people with professional expertise and technical capacity for the board of directors and senior management.
5) *Remuneration committee*: according to principle 3/2, the board of directors must form a committee concerned with bonuses, its primary role being the development of policies and regulations for granting compensation and bonuses.

---

42  Vikash Kumar Sinha and Marika Arena, 'Manifold Conceptions of the Internal Auditing of Risk Culture in the Financial Sector' (2018) 1 *Journal of Business Ethics* 13.

It should be noted that, in Kuwait, the formation of committees is the responsibility of the board of directors and is not limited to the aforementioned committees. It should also be noted that the 2015 Code made some of these committees voluntary, whilst some remain mandatory. However, in terms of good corporate governance policies, companies who form these committees are more likely to be professionally managed.

### 9.3.5 *'No One Size Fits All' Principle*

It is true that one size does not fit all listed companies in the corporate governance regime. Small companies with limited resources would avoid the statutory requirements or try to withdraw from being listed on stock exchanges which would affect the growth of the economy as well as the stock exchange and the small companies.

Small companies are the engines of economic growth. Small, listed companies are important to the future development in the growth of the economy.[43] Complying with compulsory rules is onerous for small and medium-sized listed companies.[44] It is also a major challenge for small businesses because of the costs involved.[45] If small companies are not encouraged to list their shares, they cannot receive funding from the stock exchange, which is a flexible source of capital, and this process would avoid bad debts.[46]

## 9.4 Corporate Governance in the UK

In the UK, corporate governance is regulated by a mixture of laws, rules, and codes, such as the Company Act 2006, the Bribery Act 2010, the Financial Services and Market Act 2000 (FSMA), listing rules that apply the Corporate Governance Code, business principles, the Takeover Code, and the Stewardship Code 2010. Some of these laws, rules, and codes are mentioned in later sections because of their effect on corporate governance in the UK. However, this section discusses the UK Corporate Governance Code.

Among the most important codes relating to corporate governance are the UK Corporate Governance Code 2018 and the UK Stewardship

---

43 <www.theqca.com/article_assets/articledir_210/105491/QCAResponseFRC_Improving _Quality_Reporting_Smaller_Listed_AIM_Quoted_Companies_Jul15.pdf>.
44 Ibid.
45 Ibid.
46 <www.ft.com/cms/s/0/1a905c28-0aad-11e5-98d3-00144feabdc0.html#axzz3rH8e9NO7>.

Code 2018, the latter of which is related to institutional investors.[47] These investors can play a role in enforcing the corporate governance code and this will be shown later. Both are published by the Financial Reporting Council (FRC).

In 2013, the FSA's functions were taken over by the Financial Conduct Authority (FCA) and the Prudential Regulation Authority (PRA), as a result of which the FSA was renamed the FCA according to the Financial Services Act 2012, which amended the FSMA 2000. The FCA is responsible for the 'conduct of business regulation' for all firms, while the PRA is responsible for prudential authority firms (such as banks, insurance, Lloyds of London, building societies, and some investment firms) for 'supervision' of prudential issues. 'Conduct of business regulation' means protecting investors, policing the market, and promoting competition and protection for consumers.[48]

The FCA is fully funded by the companies that it regulates,[49] and it works independently of the government. The Treasury appoints the board that manages the FCA. The Finance Reporting Council (FRC) is responsible for publishing the Corporate Governance Code. The FRC is a non-profit organisation in the form of a company limited by guarantee. Funded partly by government and partly by industry, the FRC's board is appointed by the Secretary of State for Business. The FRC is responsible for promoting high-quality corporate governance, and it is an independent regulator.[50]

Many of the FRC's functions, including setting the UK Corporate Governance Code, are recognised in statute under the Company Act 2006 and the Companies (Audit, Investigations and Community Enterprise) Act 2004.[51] In April 2013, both the FCA and the FRC signed a memorandum of understanding (MoU) for cooperation and coordination. This sets out their different responsibilities as follows: '3 – The FRC is responsible for promoting high quality corporate governance and reporting to foster investment, while the FCA is responsible for the integrity of the provision of financial services to users'.[52]

---

47 Institutional investors can play a significant role in corporate governance developments and enforcement, as can be seen clearly in the UK and the US, but they do not act as owners; Christine Mallin (n 262) 367.
48 <http://uk.practicallaw.com/7-503-5430?service=fs#a857525>.
49 <www.fca.org.uk/about>.
50 <www.frc.org.uk/>.
51 <http://frc.org.uk/Our-Work/Publications/FRC-Board/Memorandum-of-Understanding -between-the-Financial.aspx>.
52 Ibid.

## 9.5  Corporate Governance in the US

There is no formal corporate governance code in the US. Corporate governance requirements are formed by various federal laws, such as:

- The Sarbanes-Oxley Act of 2002 (Sarbanes-Oxley Act).
- The Dodd-Frank Wall Street Reform and the Consumer Protection Act (Dodd-Frank Act).
- The Federal Securities Law.
- Regulations, rules, and other guidance promulgated by the Security and Exchange Commission.
- The listing standards of registered stock exchanges that require listed companies to maintain specified corporate governance rules.

## 9.6  Corporate Governance in Kuwait

The Capital Market Authority in Kuwait enacted a series of Acts from 2013 to 2015. The 2013 Code is the first Kuwaiti Corporate Governance Code. In 2015, the code replaced several provisions from previous codes. For instance, according to the 2013 Code, compliance was mandatory, and failure to comply was a breach of Securities Law No 7 of 2010. Moreover, a company must send a quarterly report to the Kuwaiti Capital Market Authority confirming that it has complied with all the corporate governance provisions; this is now in its annual report. The 2015 code added the concept of 'comply or explain'.

Corporate governance in Kuwait is lacking in two areas. First, coverage of the various areas of corporate governance, such as risk management, is inadequate. Second, the methods of enforcement of the corporate governance provisions that do exist can be improved.

### 9.6.1  Existing Corporate Governance Provisions Relating to Listed Companies

In Kuwait, various laws affect companies. As in the UK, some laws apply to all companies, as do the Company Act 2006 in the UK and the Companies Act 2016 in Kuwait. Other laws apply only to listed companies and are enforced by the capital market authorities in the respective countries, such as the FCA in the UK.

For example, according to Article 1 of the Kuwait Companies Act 2016, this Act shall apply to companies incorporated in Kuwait or headquartered in Kuwait. Consequently, non-Kuwaiti listed companies are subject only to laws, rules, and codes of the Kuwaiti Stock Exchange. If a UK company is listed on the Kuwaiti Stock Exchange, it must comply with the rules of the Kuwait Stock Exchange. The company's activities are in the UK even though it is listed on the Kuwaiti Stock Exchange. As a result, its activities must follow Kuwaiti company law, although its listing must comply with the laws, rules, and code of the London Stock Exchange. Consequently, the Kuwaiti company does not have to comply with the UK Company Act 2006.

These laws address issues of corporate governance either directly or indirectly. For example, the liabilities of directors and the rights of shareholders are usually contained in corporate law, while other aspects of corporate governance form part of statutory instruments, such as rules and codes, and legislation affecting listed companies. Sometimes, there is an overlap between the two types of legislation, namely corporate and securities legislation. When a company is listed in the same country as it is incorporated, the company will be subject to both sets of legislation. However, if a company is listed on a stock exchange in a jurisdiction other than where it is incorporated, the jurisdiction in which the stock exchange is located can hold it accountable only according to statutory instruments that apply to that stock exchange.

### 9.6.2 *Kuwait Corporate Governance Code*

Kuwait adopted a principles-based approach to corporate governance rather than a rules-based approach with the enactment of the Kuwaiti Code 2015. This means that companies whose shares are listed on the main markets of the Kuwait Stock Exchange do not have to comply with the Code. However, if they decide not to comply, they must explain to their shareholders the reasons for non-compliance.

Furthermore, they must include in their annual report and accounts two statements:

1) An explanation about how the company has applied the main and supporting principles.
2) A statement about whether the company has complied with the provisions throughout the year covered by the report.

If the company has not complied with all provisions or has complied with them for only part of the year, the company must state its reasons for non-compliance.

The 'comply or explain' approach is a key feature of the Kuwait 2015 Code. However, Kuwait has a different approach to corporate governance and its enforcement. In Kuwait, compliance is mandatory in some respects, and failure to comply is a breach of Securities Law No 7 of 2010. However, not all compliance issues are mandatory with some being voluntary under the comply or explain regime.

### 9.6.3  Corporate Governance Principles in Kuwait

In Kuwait, the Corporate Governance Code is extensive. Both Resolution No 25 of 2013, as well as the Kuwait Corporate Governance Code 2015, include 11 principles that aim to:

- Strengthen board composition.
- Establish clear roles and responsibilities.
- Recruit highly qualified candidates for boards of directors and senior management.
- Safeguard integrity in financial reporting.
- Require sound systems of risk management and internal controls.
- Promote ethical standards and responsible conduct.
- Ensure timely and high-quality disclosure.
- Recognise the legitimate interests of stakeholders.
- Encourage enhanced performance.
- Stress the importance of social responsibility.[53]
- Protect the rights of shareholders.[54]

## 9.7  Diversity of Enforcement Methods of Corporate Governance Principles

Companies fail because they are poorly managed by the board of directors or because of external risks and factors (the economy, interest rates, exchange rates, etc). Accordingly, the law aims to encourage good management by the board.

The traditional ways of enforcing corporate governance principles are not suitable for the real world today. The world needs a new framework for the enforcement of corporate governance principles. Through rules and codes, the securities laws can help to form this framework. There is a

---

53 That could happen, for example, when the company is working to achieve a balance between the objectives of the company and the community in the context of assistance in providing job opportunities, supporting small projects, protecting the environment from pollution, contributing to the reduction of the negative phenomena in society, etc. according to Kuwaiti Corporate Governance Code 2013.

54 An example of such protection is not to have shareholder funds expropriated by the managers of a company.

diversity of enforcement methods. Different aspects of corporate governance are enforced in different ways. Some are enforced by corporate law,[55] while others are dealt with by securities laws[56] and delegated legislation in the forms of rules[57] and voluntary[58] and mandatory codes.[59]

Voluntary compliance has advantages for businesses. The nature of business requires a flexible and easily developed means of enforcement because one size does not fit all. Diversity in enforcement, including rules and codes, could solve problems related to compliance. Preventing the corporate failures that have afflicted large companies all over the world starts with proper regulation and laws. Thereafter, a diversity of enforcement methods as applied by a regulatory authority can ensure proper compliance by companies. However, the code will constantly need to be reviewed and updated to keep pace with the methods employed by companies.

It is unrealistic to try to fill these gaps with mandatory rules and regulations. A diversity of enforcement is required that is partly voluntary[60] and partly mandatory, which is the approach adopted in the UK. Seventy countries have adopted corporate governance codes in some form or another.[61]

55  Kuwait Companies Law 2013; UK Company Act 2006.
56  UK FSMA 2000 and UK FSA 2012; Kuwaiti Law No 7 of 2010.
57  Listing rules; disclosure rules; FCA's principles for business (the principles).
58  UK Corporate Governance Code 2018.
59  Kuwait Corporate Governance Code 2015.
60  Such voluntary enforcement is generally referred to as 'comply or explain' and is underpinned by a regulatory framework that asks companies to send a report annually to the shareholders about the extent to which the principles have been adhered to and, if not, why not.
61  Brian Cheffins, 'Corporate Governance LLM Cambridge, an Introduction Part 2 (3CL)' (Cambridge University iTunes).

# Conclusion

This book has considered the topic of securities trading and securities laws. It does not purport to be an exhaustive study dealing with every aspect relating to securities law. However, it has tried to explain the main features of this field of study to equip the reader with a broad understanding of the topic. Further study of the topic is encouraged, especially for those who wish to work in the field of securities law.

It is clear from the discussion that each country approaches the subject differently, based on its own experiences in the field. Corporate and government scandals have caused much harm to individuals, particularly investors, and as such, more regulation is needed. However, complex regulation and overly strict rules and laws tend to hamper economic growth and development. It is, thus, up to each legislature and regulatory authority to find the requisite balance in this regard.

Countries like Kuwait can benefit from looking at the experiences of countries such as the UK and the US to avoid potential pitfalls and problems. However, this needs to be done bearing in mind the socio-economic climate in the country, as well as the need to diversify the economy of Kuwait. Whilst attracting foreign investment to Kuwait should be a priority, this needs to be balanced with growing the economy for the benefit of the broader population. Several improvements to the enforcement system, such as expert judges and criminal authorities who are experts in financial matters, will assist in this regard. This will increase the level of confidence and credibility.

In addition, the field of securities law will need to constantly be updated and improved as businesses grow and evolve in the future. Legislatures and regulatory authorities should keep a close watch on developments in the markets and business community to note any negative trends or possible abuses. Vigilant enforcement with stricter penalties will reduce the risk of any major financial crisis.

DOI: 10.4324/9781003301875-11

# Index

*Note*: Page numbers **bold** indicate tables in the text and references following "n" refer notes.